The American Terrorist:

Everything You Need to Know to be a Subject Matter Expert

Authors:

Dr. Terry Oroszi and Dr. David Ellis

Greylander Press

The American Terrorist:

Everything You Need to Know to be a Subject Matter Expert

© *Greylander Press*

ISBN: 978-0-9821683-2-5

This book is dedicated to the men and women that risk their lives every day to keep us safe.

Table of Contents

Preface 14
Chapter One 16
   Terrorism Defined 16
Chapter Two 22
   Domestic Terror Organizations 22
   The Alabama Free Militia 26
   The Alternative Right 26
   Alpha 66 and Omega 7 26
   Animal Liberation Front 28
   Antifa 28
   Army of God 29
   Aryan Nations 30
   Black Panther Party /Black Liberation Army 20
   The Covenant, the Sword, and the Arm of the Lord 31
   Earth Liberation Front 31
   Fuerzas Armadas De Liberacion Nacional Puertorriquena 32
   Hutaree 33
   Jam'iyyat Ul-Ilam Is-Saheeh 34
   The Jewish Defense League 34
   Ku Klux Klan 34
   May 19th Communist Organization 35
   National Alliance 36
   The National Socialist Movement 36
   The American Nazi Party 37
   Operation Save America 37
   Phineas Priesthood 38
   Proud Boys 38
   Public Enemy Number 1 39
   Republic of New Africa 40
   Revolutionary People's Group 40
   Sovereign Citizens Movement 41

Symbionese Liberation Army 42
United Freedom Front 43
Weather Underground Organization 43
Chapter Two Summary 44
Chapter Three 46
Terror Cells in the United States 46
Alaska SC Cell 47
Boston Terror Cell 47
Columbus Terror Cell 47
D.C. Five / Pakistani Five Cell 48
Florida Cell 48
Fort Dix Plot / Fort Dix Five 48
ISIS NY Cell 49
Jihadist Cell 49
Lackawanna Six / Buffalo Six Cell 49
Miami Seven / Liberty City Seven Cell 50
Newburgh Four 50
NY Terror Cell 51
Raleigh Jihad Group / Quantico Attack 51
Revolution Muslim 51
Texas Cartoon Terrorists 51
The Portland Seven Cell 52
Toledo Terror Cell 52
Virginia Jihad Cell 53
Chapter Three Summary... 53
Chapter Four 54
International Terrorist Organizations 54
Abu Sayyaf Group 57
Al Fuqra 58
Al Haramain Islamic Foundation 58
Al-Qaeda 59
Al-Qaida in the Arabian Peninsula 60
Al-Qaeda in Iraq 61

Al-Shabaab 61
Ansar Al-Islam 62
Hamas 62
Hezbollah 63
Iranian Islamic Revolutionary Guard Corps 64
Islamic State of Iraq And Syria 64
Jabhat Al-Nusra / Nusra Front 66
Jaish-E-Mohammed 67
Lashkar-E-Tayyiba 67
Taliban 68
Pakistan Taliban / Tehrik-E-Taliban 69
Tamil Tigers/ Liberation Tigers of Tamil Eelam 69
Chapter Four Summary 70
Chapter Five 71
Education, Profession, and Marital Status 71
Education 71
Profession 74
Marital Status 77
Chapter Five Summary 80
Chapter Six 81
Mindset of A Terrorist 81
Economy 83
Poverty 85
Political Freedom 87
Race, Gender, And Sexuality 90
Religion 93
Awlaki Influence 97
Social Services as A Solution 98
Chapter Six Summary 99
Chapter Seven 101
Is Your Neighbor a Terrorist 101
Quick Facts about The Top Ten States 102
The Citizenship of American Terrorists 106

The U.S. Born Citizens 108
Naturalized Citizens 110
Chapter Seven Summary 113
Chapter Eight 114
The American Female Terrorist 114
Women's Role in Terrorism 115
The Demographics of a Woman Terrorist 116
The Women of American Terrorism 118
The Statistics 118
Age (At the Time of the Crime) 118
Allegiance 119
Education 119
Marital Status and Children 120
Mental Health Issues 121
Sentence/Status 121
Terror Timeline.. 121
Historical Female Terrorists 122
Rachel Pendergraft 122
Lisa Turner 123
Kathy Ainsworth 123
Joanne Chesimard 123
Diana Oughton 124
Angela Shannon 125
Shelley Shannon 125
Susan Stern 126
Chapter Eight Summary 127
Chapter Nine 129
The American Male Terrorist 129
Terror TimeLine 130
The Age of Male Terrorists 130
Allegiance 132
Education 134
Married/Children 134

VII

Male Terrorist Mental Health 134
Sentence/Status 135
Chapter Nine Summary 136
Chapter Ten 138
Recognizing a Developing Terrorist 138
Historical Terrorist Profiling 139
The Profile 140
Other Interesting Findings 147
Chapter Ten Summary 148
Chapter Eleven 149
American Terrorists and the Military 149
Terrorists Who Served in the Army 151
Terrorists Who Served in the Marines 158
Terrorists Who Served in the Navy 161
Terrorist Who Served in the U.S. Air Force 163
Terrorists Targeting the Military 164
Chapter Eleven Summary 168
Chapter Twelve 169
Behind Bars 169
Official Charges 170
FBI Involvement 179
Prison Location 180
Sentencing 181
The Targets of American Terrorists 183
Crimes Involving Violence 185
Weapons Used 186
Recidivism 187
Deradicalization 189
Chapter Twelve Summary 190
Chapter Thirteen 192
Prevention Strategies and Federal Policies 192
The Use of the Terrorist Profile as a Tool for Prevention .193
De-Radicalization and Disengagement 194

Federal Policies Related To Terrorism 195
The Biological Weapons Anti-Terrorism Act Of 1989 196
Executive Order 12947 197
Omnibus Counter-Terrorism Act of 1995 198
U.S. Antiterrorism and Effective Death Penalty Act Of 1996 198
Executive Order 13224 199
USA PATRIOT Act and the USA Freedom Act 199
Homeland Security Act of 2002, Pub. L. 107-296 201
Border Protection, Anti-Terrorism, and Illegal Immigration Control Act Of 2005 (Sensenbrenner Bill) 201
Detainee Treatment Act of 2005 201
Military Commissions Act Of 2006 201
Chapter Thirteen Summary 202
References 205
Index 221

List of Figures

Figure 1: American Terrorists Aligned with International Terrorist Organizations 55

Figure 2: Male American Terrorists Relationship Status 78

Figure 3: Female American Terrorists Relationship Status 78

Figure 4: Male American Terrorists and Social Class or Position 86

Figure 5: Female American Terrorists and Social Class or Position.. 86

Figure 6: American-Born, Multi-Generational Terrorists in Each of the Indicated Ethnic Groups 92

Figure 7: Female Multi-Generational, American-Born Terrorists in Each Of The Indicated Ethnic Groups 92

Figure 8: The Distribution of Muslims and Non-Muslims. 95

Figure 9: World Map Showing The Location Of Terrorist Training Camps.. 96

Figure 10: American Terrorists Who Trained At Terrorist Camps Located in the Countries 96

Figure 11: The Number of Terrorists Residing in States at the Time of Arrest 104

Figure 12: U.S. Map Showing American Terrorists Who Resided In Each State At The Time Of Their Arrest 107

Figure 13: Distribution of Citizens 108

Figure 14: The Number of American Terrorists with Parents from the Countries or Territories 109

Figure 15: World Map Showing the Home Countries of the Parents of U.S. Born Terrorists 110

Figure 16: The Number of American-Born Terrorists with Parents from Each of the Countries or Territories 111

Figure 17: Naturalized American Terrorists with Parents from Each of the Indicated Countries or Territories 112

Figure 18: The Ages of American Females at the Time of Arrest 119

Figure 19: American Females and Their Proclaimed Allegiances 120

Figure 20: The Number of American Females Charged and the Year of Arrest 122

Figure 21: The Number of American Males Charged and the Years of Arrest 131

Figure 22: The Ages of American Males at the Time of Arrest ... 131

Figure 23: American Male Citizens Aligned with Domestic Terror Organizations 133

Figure 24: American Male Citizens Aligned with International Terror Organizations 136

Figure 25: Profile Marker #1 141

Figure 26: Profile Marker #2 142

Figure 27: Profile Marker #3 143

Figure 28: Strengthening Profile Marker #3 144

Figure 29: Profile Marker #4 145

Figure 30: The FBI 180

Figure 31: U.S. Map Showing the Number of American Terrorists Held In Prisons in Each State 181

Figure 32: The Number of Terrorists Held in Prisons 182

Figure 33: The Number American Female's Jail Sentence 182

Figure 34: American Terrorists with the Indicated Alternative Sentences 183

Figure 35: The Number of American Males Convicted of Acts Related to Terrorism and Their Sentence Lengths. 184

Figure 36: American Terrorists and Their Indicated Targets 185

Figure 37: The Distribution of Violent and Non-Violent Crimes 186

Figure 38: American Terrorists and Their Weapons...................187

List of Tables

Table 1: Domestic Terror Organizations 24

Table 2: American Terrorists and Their Majors 74

Table 3: Terrorists in the Top Fourteen Industries 76

Table 4: American Terrorists Relationships 79

Table 5: Gender and Terrorism 91

Table 6: Top Ten States. 102

Table 7: Top Cities 103

Table 8: The Citizenship of American Terrorist 107

Table 9: Federal Crimes of Terrorism 177

XIII

Preface

What much of the population knows about terrorists stems from gossip, hearsay, generalized data, and assumptions. Common expectations about terrorists include that they are uneducated, young, of Middle Eastern descent, unemployed or poor, and lastly, evil. Three years ago, we set out to collect data on the American citizens, both men and women, charged with acts related to terrorism (for specific charges see Chapter 12), so we could provide the facts and help the public understand the true profile of an American terrorist.

The chances of an act of terror affecting an average American citizen are small, but the fear of terrorism is inescapable. To most people, terrorism seems to occur randomly. Understanding the real data, discovering its patterns, and generating a true terrorist profile will reduce the apparent randomness and lack of control.

Defining the terrorist profile is one step toward taking control back from those who seek to change our way of life.

In addition to the collection of five hundred and nineteen men and woman charged with terrorism, we were able to gather information from current literature that supported or enhanced the work. The necessary information was gleamed from court records, government and academic databases, books, newspapers and other media sources.

In an age where "fake news" has become commonplace, one might question the legitimacy of using media to obtain facts, but those sources are the best for finding personal information on an individual, such as their level of education or marital status. Court records rarely have such information. The authors worked diligently to provide the readers with the most accurate information possible; however, sources can be wrong, and sometimes that data is populated in several places, giving the illusion of multiple sources. This research is not an attempt to single out or cause pain to any individual or group.

For ease of identification and to highlight the number of American citizens born in the USA, individuals in this book are identified by their birth name first, and the names given after conversion to Islam in parenthesis.

It is only fair to say this research was only possible because of the men and women that did similar research and made their work public so that others could build on it.

Chapter One

Terrorism Defined

It was an 80-mile drive from Mesquite, Nevada to Las Vegas, one that retiree Stephen Paddock made in the fall of 2017. His Mandalay Bay hotel suite overlooked the Harvest country music festival, so he could enjoy the music without mingling with the crowd of 22,000 fans. Over the past week, he had spent his time gambling, much like many Las Vegas visitors, but Paddock was the exception, gambling was not his main desire on this trip.

Paddock could barely walk around due to the stash of weapons in his room. The collection included 47 guns, many with semi-automatic firing ability. On that warm Sunday evening, he looked out onto the crowd and, without missing a beat, picked up one of his semi-automatic weapons and fired into the gathering, killing fifty-nine and injuring 527 concert-goers.

People watched with horror and deemed this man, responsible for the worst mass shooting in U.S. history, a terrorist, but they were wrong. Incidents like this muddle our understanding of terrorism, and so before we can discuss such a complex topic, we need to establish an operational definition of terrorism.

For this book, we will merge three definitions from the sources that are cited most often by terrorism experts: The United States Code, Title 18 (Title 18); The United States Federal Bureau of Investigation (FBI); and the United States Department of Defense (DOD).

Title 18 is the criminal and penal code of the federal government of the United States. Subjects covered by Title 18 include biological and chemical weapons as well as terrorism. Title 18, Crimes and Criminal Procedure defines international terrorism as:

> *"...activities that involve violent acts or acts dangerous to human life that is a violation of the criminal law..., appear to be intended to intimidate or coerce a civilian population, influence the policy of a government by intimidation or coercion, or to affect the conduct of a government by mass destruction, assassination, or kidnapping; and occur primarily outside the territorial jurisdiction of the United States..." (18 U.S.C. § 2331)*

Domestic terrorism is defined the same way, but the acts occur primarily within the territorial jurisdiction of the United States. Note that the objective is only defined in general terms: to intimidate or coerce or affect the conduct of government. No specific objectives are given. Most of the definition is clear, but the difference between international and domestic terrorism can be confusing. If training, planning, obtaining materials or other activities directly or indirectly related to the terror act took place in the United States, then it becomes a domestic act of terror. If the activities happened outside of the United States, it becomes an act of international terrorism. Al-Qaeda, for example, planned the September 11, 2001, attack on the United States from outside of the country's boundaries, and so it meets the definition of an international terrorist act. The bombing of the Boston Marathon by the Tsarnaev brothers in 2013 was planned and executed in the United States and is therefore domestic terrorism.

The Code of Federal Regulations (CFR) assigns lead-agency responsibility for investigating acts of terrorism to the Federal Bureau of Investigation and defines terrorism as:

> *"...the unlawful use of force and violence against persons or property to intimidate or coerce a government, the civilian population, or any segment thereof, in furtherance of political or social objectives" (28 CFR § 0.85(l)).*

Here, the definition specifies that the intent of terrorism is to advance political or social objectives. The FBI uses the same language as Title 18 to distinguish between domestic and international terrorism (1), but expands on the difference to better clarify. International acts of terrorism are inspired by or associated with designated foreign terrorist organizations or nations, while domestic acts are inspired by or associated with primarily U.S.-based movements that espouse extremist ideologies of a political, religious, social, racial, or environmental nature (2).

The DOD's definition of terrorism is as follows:

> *"The unlawful use of violence or threat of violence, often motivated by religious, political, or other ideological beliefs, to instill fear and coerce governments or societies in pursuit of goals that are usually political (3)."*

This definition provides examples for the motivation and objectives of terrorism without limiting the definition to those objectives. The DOD does not openly provide a distinction between international and domestic terrorism. Combining these three, commonly-cited definitions, we can create an operational definition of terrorism:

> *"The illegal use of force, violence, or threat of violence for the purpose of intimidating, instilling fear, and coercing a civilian or government entity with the goal of advancing religious, political, or ideological objectives. "*

Thus, the terrorist seeks to induce a change in the ideology or set of beliefs, principles, or ethics, of its civilian or government target. The type of crime and scale of its outcome should not be used to determine if a crime is an act of terrorism. A secular terrorist group, for example, might use violence to advance their ideology, but will likely be selective in what type of violence they use because they want to avoid losing political power and support. Certain actions could damage the organization's reputation and limit what they could accomplish through political means.

Religiously motivated groups may try to inflict as many casualties as possible because their belief in an afterlife renders the loss of life irrelevant. They might keep such violence away from their territory, however, because killing or destroying the homes of their members will not ingratiate the leaders to the followers.

In July 2016 there were several events involving the police shooting African-American male youths. This perceived injustice against the African American community stirred one individual, Micah Johnson, to open fire on the police in Dallas, Texas, killing five and wounding seven officers. Many news media outlets, such as CNN called this an act of terror, but the desire of an African American male who showed interest in radical black-power organizations, to shoot white police officers is a hate crime. The FBI describes a hate crime as:

"a criminal offense against a person or property motivated, in whole or in part by an offender's bias against a race, religion, disability, sexual orientation, ethnicity, gender, or gender identity (4)."

A hate crime is a traditional offense like murder or arson with an added element of bias. The sentence cannot exceed ten years. It is typically used as an add-on charge to increase the punishment for another offense. Interestingly, in Islamic Law, the same law that covers hate crimes includes terrorism. There is no distinction between political, ideological or religious goals because, in Sharia law, they are one and the same (5).

The year 1968 has been identified as the year of modern international terrorism (6). At the time, there were eleven foreign terrorist organizations (FTO) operating in the world (Ibid), whereas today, there are sixty-seven FTOs in the world (7). In the 1970s domestic security crimes were renamed as terrorism crimes (8). It was the Anti-Terrorism and Effective Death Penalty Act of 1996 (Pub. LAW 104-132) that introduced the country to terrorism as a crime in the United States.

As recent as 1983 the FBI would not investigate a terrorist act unless it had more than one person involved (8). Today, the majority of successful terrorism prosecutions in the U.S. have been against American citizens that have aligned themselves with international groups like al-Qaeda, al-Shabaab, al-Nusra, and the Islamic State (ISIS).

Chapter One Summary

This chapter identified three definitions of domestic terrorism that boil down to violent acts that violate state and federal laws happening on U.S. soil. The terrorists commit a violent act such as killing, kidnapping, or mass destruction, with the goal of intimidating people to change policies or laws. If the individuals or groups committing the acts of violence are doing so because the victims do not follow their personal or religious beliefs or can be used as a tool for political gain, then the chances are they are acts of terrorism. If an individual pulls out a gun and fires at school kids or co-workers, the individual is not likely to be prosecuted as a terrorist.

If an American born terrorist plan and train for an attack in the U.S. while not on U.S. soil, they are an international terrorist. If a foreign national plans, trains, or uses resources found in the U.S., they would be considered a domestic terrorist. If the planning, training, and execution of the violent act occurred both on U.S. soil and abroad, the judicial system would have to decide where it fits.

Terrorism as a crime is not new; however, federal laws prosecuting terrorists are new. While most terrorists are charged with crimes other than terrorism, or in addition to terrorism, the acts remain quite similar, they all attempt to instill fear to force change upon a population.

Chapter Two

Domestic Terror Organizations

It is easy to forget that terrorism was an American staple well before the attack on the Alfred P. Murrah Federal building in 1995, and the World Trade Center attacks in 2001. In fact, from the 1960s into the 1980s attacks were happening in the United States quite frequently, including exploding bombs, hijacking airplanes, and assignations for political gain.

Terrorist groups were formed around one goal, such as protecting the environment or protesting a specific injustice, and it was called "single-issue terrorism" (9). Domestic terror incidents greatly outnumbered international incidents (10). A conviction was difficult during that period and jail time was uncommon or relatively small (11). The domestic organizations listed in this chapter have illegally used force, violence, or the threat of violence to intimidate, instill fear, or coerce a civilian or government entity in order to advance ideological objectives, and therefore meet the definition of domestic terrorist organizations.

The U.S. government does not formally designate domestic terrorist organizations. Claiming an affiliation to a domestic terror organization, like those listed in this chapter, is not illegal. Therefore, it may not be illegal to give money or other forms of material support to a domestic terrorist group, even if the group is known for its violence and hatred of others. The First Amendment protects the right of people to associate with each other and to express their points of view.

It can be difficult to decide if a group deserves the terrorist label, especially when evaluating hate groups. If the group has a clear goal and uses premeditated, violent acts or threats of violence to further those goals, then they certainly meet the definition of terrorists. If the group condones violence, but only resorts to violence in their personal defense, are they terrorists? It seems though, that if the group condones violence, it is only a matter of time before some members make greater use of violence. Indeed, if violence is expected of the organization at every event where it promotes its ideology, is that not the same as the threat of violence?

If a group has not killed, injured, or destroyed in an effort to force others to follow its ideology, how can we label them the same as a group that does? Here, we shall call those questionable groups, "quasi-terrorist organizations." The quasi-terrorists (QTs) appear to be, or claim to be voicing their ideology without trying to force it upon others using violence or fear; however, they condone the use of violence when "necessary." Quasi-terrorist organizations say they are only demonstrating, but they insight to violence the people who oppose their ideologies. They may not be exploding targets, yet, but they have members who are fully capable of such measures.

To better explain the terror groups and their affiliations we sectioned the groups based on their goals (political, ideological or religious). In some instances, the group's goals span more than one affiliation type. An example of this is the Nazi party, as a Right Wing group they are politically motivated, but wite supremacy is an ideology. Forty-seven of the American citizens charged with acts related to terrorism self-identified as members of these groups. Some identify at a general level, such as Anti-government or Right-Wing; however, and others choose specific organizations (See Table 1).

Domestic Terror Organizations (# of terrorists from this study)

Politics:

Alpha 66 and Omega 7

The Alternative Right (Alt-Right)

Anti-government (16 terrorists)

     Sovereign Citizens Movement (6 terrorists)

Antifa

Black Panther Party (BPP)/Black Liberation Army (BLA)

Fuerzas Armadas de Liberacion Nacional Puertorriquena (FALN)

Hutaree (HUT) (3 terrorists)

May 19th Communist Organization (M19CO)

National Socialist Movement (NSM) (1 terrorist)

Republic of New Africa (RNA)

Right Wing (RW)

     The Covenant, The Sword, and the Arm of the Lord (CSA)

     Militias, like the Alabama Free Militia (AFM) (5 terrorists)

     Nazi Party (Nazi) (2 terrorists)

Revolutionary People' Group (RPG) (6 terrorists)
Symbionese Liberation Army (SLA)
United Freedom Front (UFF)
Weather Underground Organization (WUO)
Ideology:
Animal Liberation Front (ALF)
Army of God (AOG)
Earth Liberation Front (ELF)
Jewish Defense League (JDL) (4 terrorists)
White Supremacy
 Aryan Nations (AN)
 Ku Klux Klan (KKK)
 National Alliance (NA)
 National Socialist Movement (NSM) (1) terrorists)
 Nazi Party (Nazi) (2 terrorists)
 Phineas Priesthood (PP)
 Proud Boys (PB)
 Public Enemy Number 1 (PEN1)
Religion:
The Covenant, The Sword, and the Arm of the Lord (CSA)
Jam'iyyat Ul-Islam Is-Saheeh (JIS) (3 terrorists)
Operation Save America (OSA)

Table 1: Domestic Terror Organizations. Forty-seven of the Americans charged with acts related to terrorism since 9/11 self-identify as members in one of following groups. This table breaks down the groups based on the goals of the groups. In some cases, the groups align with more than one goal.

Domestic Terror Organizations

This chapter identifies each of the domestic terror organizations, including their leadership, active status, and ideology can be found below. The groups are arranged in alphabetical order.

The Alabama Free Militia (AFM)

Active: 2007 **Leadership:** Raymond Dillard **Aliases:** None **Ideology:** Political, Racist, Right-wing

Summary: The group planned an attack on Mexicans living in Birmingham. The planned to kill any government officials who attempted to stop them during the raid. Leader Raymond Dillard and five other conspirators were arrested for various charges. Among the munitions that investigators found following the arrests were One-hundred and thirty homemade grenades and an improvised grenade launcher.

The Alternative Right (Alt-Right)

The Alt-Right is not a terror organization, rather it is a set of far-right ideologies followed by groups and individuals, whose core beliefs are focused on "white identity." Members of this group include five people, three working alone, and two as partners, that were convicted of acts related to terrorism between 2003 and 2010. There is no expected age for this group; the members ranged from nineteen to eight-nine years old.

Alpha 66 and Omega 7

Active: 1960s – 1980s. **Leadership:** Alpha 66 Founder/ Leader Antonio Veciana Blanch; Omega 7 Leader Eduardo

Arocena. **Aliases:** None. **Ideology:** Political. Removal of Castro, Revolutionists for a free Cuba.

Summary: In the 1960s through the 1980s the anti-Castro terrorist organizations were rampant in the U.S. with as many as fifty-six organizations collectively responsible for the one hundred and fifty-five acts of terror in the country (11). They wanted to remove Castro from Cuba and believed that causing mayhem in the U.S., Canada, and Cuba would bring attention to their cause and aid in his ouster. There were five success-ful militarized Cuban terrorist organizations known as the Alpha-66, Omega-7, Brigade 2506, the Cuban Nationalist Movement and the Cuban National Liberation Front (Ibid). Two of the groups were trained by the U.S. Central Intelligence Agency (CIA), and are summarized here (12). The two groups were composed of Cuban expatriates in the 1960s and are examples of political terrorists. The acts of terror they com-mitted against Cubans still living in Cuba and residing in the U.S. were frequently sanctioned by the CIA (13).

In 1961 the CIA recruited and trained Cuban expatriates and sent them to unseat Castro in what is documented as the Bay of Pigs Invasion, but they failed. Sixty-six of the expatriates founded the Alpha-66 and have been targeting Cuba ever since. One method they used to target Castro was to stop tourism by bombing hotels in Cuba. Alpha-66 is the only Cuban-inspired terrorist group still operating in the U.S. today.

Omega 7 is a group that targeted Cubans that supported Castro in the 1970s and 1980s. The CIA trained some of the members during the Bay of Pigs. The group operated in Florida, New Jersey, and New York, claiming responsibility for the bombing of consulates and the assassinations of Castro-friendly Cubans in the U.S. and Canada (14). After the arrest of key members and their leader, the group became inactive.

Animal Liberation Front (ALF)

Active: 1970s – Present. **Leadership:** Leaderless organization. **Aliases:** ALF. **Ideology:** Protect Animals and the Environment. Using property damage to hinder or stop the exploitation of animals and the destruction of the environment.

Summary: The Animal Liberation Front (ALF) is the sister group to the Earth Liberation Front (ELF), both are examples of new terrorist groups operating in the United States. Together they caused nearly forty-three million dollars in damage with more than 600 acts of violence in all parts of the United States (15,16). Greenpeace and the Sea Shepherds Conservation Society were the inspiration for groups like ELF and ALF. In the 1970s the ALF was formed in Great Britain and was interested in animal rights. The U.S. branch of ALF spawned in October of 1996, with the attacking of a U.S. Forest Service truck in Oregon (Ibid). In its beginnings, the group claimed it would not harm animals or people. Acts like arson and the pipe bombing of companies in California in 2003 have earned them the label of an animal rights terrorist group (17).

Antifa

Active: 2017 – present. **Leadership:** none. **Ideology:** Political, specifically anti-fascism.

Summary: The Antifa, or antifascist movement, is dedicated to fighting against hate and suppression. This QT group claims to promote "good" activities to interfere with fascist activity and only engage in violence for self-defense, but their tactics do not always hold to those limits. In 2016, several Antifa counter protests at the University of California at Berkeley quickly turned to violence (18). Some instances may have been unprovoked and possibly premeditated. The group draws its roots from similar groups that started in Germany before World War II. Although they typically stand against groups that use violence to advance their ideology, the fact that they use violence themselves to advance their anti-fascist ideals places them on the borderline of terrorism and earns them the label of QT organization.

Army of God (AOG)

Active: 1982 – Present. **Leadership:** Michael Bray. **Aliases:** None. **Ideology:** Anti-abortion Christians using any means available.

Summary: Since the landmark Supreme Court decision, *Roe vs. Wade*, in 1973, laws restricting or further protecting reproductive rights and protecting abortion clinics, staff, and patients have been passed in several states (19). The public became acquainted with the Army of God in 1982 when members bombed an abortion clinic and kidnapped a doctor and his wife, later releasing them (20-22). Terror organizations like the Army of God commit violent acts to advance their ideology, and legalized abortion went against their core values (Ibid). The organization's devout opposition to abortion, which they viewed as murder, empowered them to do whatever it took to prevent more abortions, including bombing abortion clinics and attempting to murder physicians who worked in them (23,24).

Soon after 9/11 and the national anthrax scare, members of the Army of God initiated a nationwide hoax, sending over five hundred letters to abortion clinics with a statement that said the recipient "*was now exposed to anthrax*" (25). The group embraced social media and the internet, creating an "Army of

God" website that supports the use of violence to stop abortions.

Aryan Nations (AN)

Active: 1977 – Present. **Leadership:** Richard Girnt Butler. **Aliases:** None. **Ideology:** Neo-Nazi

Summary: The Aryan Nations was founded by the now deceased Richard Butler. It is an Idaho-based, white separatist organization believed by many to be defunct (26). They espouse a racist vision of Christianity called "Christian Identity." The Christian Identity movement believes that white Europeans are God's chosen people and all other races are inferior or even subhuman (27). The death of its founder and a court award of $6.3 million to a mother and son who were shot at and chased by AR members are said to be responsible for the demise of the Aryan Nations (Ibid).

Black Panther Party (BPP)/Black Liberation Army (BLA)

Active: 1966 – 1982. **Leadership:** Huey Newton and Bobby Seale. **Aliases:** None. **Ideology:** Black Nationalism, Anti-racism, Maoism, and Revolutionary socialism.

Summary: Huey Newton, Ph.D., was an African-American political and urban activist from California, who founded the Black Panther Party (28). He started as a criminal, but reinvented himself to be an intellectual (29). Among many charges, Dr. Newton is known best for the murder of a police officer. The Black Panther Party began fifty years ago as a political organization with the goal of changing the social consciousness of U.S. citizens and improve the civil rights of African Americans (30). The group used terrorist methods initially but became a less radical, social protest group after realizing that violence was not bringing them the success they desired (Ibid). The Black Panthers realized the value of recruiting members by meeting the social needs of the community. An example of this is their Free Breakfast for Children Program (31).

Not all of the BPP members agreed with the decision to give up their militant ways. Members that condoned the militant ideology and believed that terror was necessary to achieve their goals, formed the Black Liberation Army (32). The BLA, as a terror group, was responsible for more than twenty deaths, but claimed that their actions were for self-defense in support of the minority, and they became targets of the police and FBI (33).

The Covenant, The Sword, and the Arm of the Lord (CSA)

Active: 1970s – 1980s. **Leadership:** James Ellison. **Aliases:** CSA. **Ideology:** Far right political organization dedicated to Christian identity and survivalism.

Summary: The CSA was thrown into the spotlight in the mid 1980's when they acquired a large drum of cyanide and intended to poison water supplies in major U.S. cities (34). The group vowed to overthrow the U.S. government beginning with government workers. Additional terrorist activities include burning a church in Missouri, firebombing a synagogue in Indiana, and attempting to bomb a gas pipeline in Illinois.

Earth Liberation Front (ELF)

Active: 1993 – Present. **Leadership:** No defined leadership. **Aliases:** The Elves; ELF. **Ideology:** The use of economic sabotage and guerrilla warfare to protect the environment.

Summary: Leaderless groups like ELF and ALF, encourage individuals or small cells to engage in acts of violence without a network or support system (15). The lack of leadership aids in avoiding detection and prosecution of the members while the group's ideology preserves a feeling of inclusiveness for its members (Ibid). Since September 11, 2001, Elf has become the most destructive terrorist group in the United States (Ibid).

"Let this be a lesson to all greedy multinational corporations who do not respect their ecosystems. The elves are watching." - Earth Liberation Front (35)

Fuerzas Armadas de Liberacion Nacional Puertorriquena (FALN)

Active: 1974 – 1983 **Leadership**: Filiberto Ojeda Rios **Aliases**: FALN. **Ideology**: Independence for Puerto Rico, Marxism-Leninism, Communism.

Summary: The Armed forces of Puerto Rican National Liberation (FALN) carried out more than one hundred and thirty bombings in the U.S. to draw attention to the colonial condition of Puerto Rico (11). Sixteen members were convicted of conspiracy to commit robbery, conspiracy to bomb-making, sedition, and firearm and explosives violations in 1980 (Ibid). President Bill Clinton pardoned fifteen of them in 1999, under the condition that they no longer participate in such activities. President Barack Obama commuted the sentence of the remaining member in 2017.

Hutaree (HUT)

Active: 2006-present **Leadership:** David Stone **Aliases:** None. **Ideology:** Christian Warriors, ideology of the Christian

Patriot movement.

Summary: The group formed in early 2006. They were a militia group based near Adrian, Michigan, that adhered to the ideology of the Christian Patriot movement. Arrested in 2010, Joshua Clough, Joshua Matthew Stone, and David Brian Stone Sr. were plotting to kill a police officer, and then bomb the funeral.

Jam'iyyat Ul-Islam Is-Saheeh (JIS)

Active: 2005 **Leadership:** Kevin James **Aliases:** Authentic Assembly of God **Ideology:** al-Qaeda of California

Summary: In 2005, four friends known as the "Torrance Four" were indicted for their alleged roles in a terrorist plot to attack U.S. military facilities, Israeli government facilities and Jewish synagogues in the Los Angeles area. The leader, Kevin James (Shaykh Shahaab Murshid), founded the JIS while in prison in 1997 and directed its actions on the outside. Another member, U.S. citizen Lavar Haley Washington, joined the JIS in prison and recruited two more members, U.S. citizen Gregory Vernon Patterson and resident Hammad Riaz Samana when he was released. They named themselves Jam'iyyat Ul-Islam Is-Saheeh, or the Assembly of Authentic Islam. The men considered themselves the "al-Qaeda of California." The four ex-convicts were charged in 2005 with plotting a series of attacks on military and Jewish targets in Los Angeles. They are classified here as a domestic terror group because they named their organization and instead of pledging their allegiance with the existing terrorist organization, they acted independently, thinking of themselves as al-Qaeda of California.

The Jewish Defense League (JDL)

Active: 1969 – Present. **Leadership:** Rabbi Meir Kahane. **Aliases:** None. **Ideology:** a violent form of anti-Arab, Jewish nationalism.

Summary: The Southern Poverty Law Center (SPLC) defined the JDL as a radical organization that preaches a violent form of anti-Arab, Jewish nationalism. Headquartered in New York, the Jewish Defense League was led by Meir Kahane in 1969 (36). Kahane was charged with the kidnapping of a Soviet diplomat, the bombing of the Iraqi embassy in Washington, and arms dealing. In response to anti-Semitic feelings in the U.S. and overseas, the Jewish Defense League was formed to assist young Jewish individuals in defending themselves and their culture. Betar was another Jewish militant group active in the U.S., but not as established as the JDL (37).

In 2002, Dr. Robert Goldstein, a Jewish podiatrist, his wife and two partners plotted to bomb Islamic mosques, centers, and schools in Florida and planned to kill fleeing worshippers and responding officers. They were alleged to be JDL members.

> *"To turn the other cheek is not a Jewish concept."* — Rabbi Meir Kahane

Ku Klux Klan (KKK)

Active: 1866 – Present. **Leadership:** Calvin Jones, John B. Kennedy, James R. Crowe, Frank O. McCord, John C. Lester, and Richard R. Reed. The current leader is David Duke. **Aliases:** The Klan and for a short time Kuklux Clan. **Ideology:** Neo-Nazi.

Summary: Currently, the Ku Klux Klan is identified as an international terrorist group, but its origins are in Pulaski, Tennessee, where six Confederate veterans upset with the outcome of the civil war, set out to suppress and victimize newly freed slaves by using violence against African American leaders. With the help of federal law enforcement, the KKK was suppressed in 1871 (38). There was a clan rebirth in 1915 and it flourished nationwide in the early and mid-1920s. It was deep-rooted in local Protestant communities and opposed Catholics and Jews (39). In the 1950's, small, local, unconnected groups using the KKK name began to appear, focused on obstructing the Civil Rights Movement and often using violence and murder to suppress activists. The Southern Poverty Law Center estimates the KKK to be 6,000 – 8,000 in total membership. The KKK considers themselves moral, upstanding Christians; however, Christian denominations have officially denounced the KKK (40). The violent practices and threats of violence by the KKK are well known and deserving of the terrorist label.

In 1995, Don Black and David Duke's ex-wife Chloê Hardin created an online presence known as Stormfront, which has become a prominent forum for hate groups (41).

May 19th Communist Organization (M19CO)

Active: 1978 – 1985. **Leadership:** Silvia Baraldini. **Aliases:** M19CO, May 19 Communist Coalition, May 19 Communist, Red Guerrilla Resistance, the Revolutionary Fighting Group, the Armed Resistance Unit. **Ideology:** Political. Anti-capitalism, Communism, and Left-wing terrorism.

Summary: The members of the Weather Underground Organization, the Black Liberation Army, The Black Panthers and the Republic of New Africa (RNA) formed the now-defunct

May 19th Communist Organization. The name, M19CO, was derived from the birthdays of Vietnamese leader Ho Chi Minh and Malcolm X. It was a US-based revolutionary group with the objective of freeing political prisoners in U.S. prisons. They sought to appropriate capitalist wealth (armed robberies) to fund the third stage, which was a series of bombings and terrorist attacks.

National Alliance

Active: 1974 – Present. **Leadership:** Founder William Pierce. The current leader, Erich Gliebe. **Aliases:** National Youth Alliance (NYA) and some members formed a splinter group, National Vanguard, and that group split to become the Nationalist Coalition and the European Americans United. **Ideology:** Neo-Nazi, the genocide of Jews and other races.

Summary: The National Alliance was the leading neo-Nazi organization in the 1990's and is still operating today (42). It is one of the most dangerous and feared neo-Nazi groups because of its successful recruiting and criminal record of violence and robbery (43). Timothy McVeigh was influenced by the Christian Identity movement and by "The Turner Diaries," a book written by William Pierce, the founder of the National Alliance (44).

The National Socialist Movement (NSM)

Active: 1994 – Present. **Leadership:** Founder and leader Jeff Schoep. **Aliases:** None. **Ideology:** Political and Neo-Nazi

Summary: Previously known as the National Socialist American Workers Freedom Movement and rooted in the original American Nazi party, the National Socialist Movement is the largest neo-Nazi organization in the country. It boasts a recruitment wing dedicated to teenagers (Viking Youth Corps), a women's division, a skinhead division, a white-supremacist social network site (New Saxon), and its own hate rock music label (NSM88 Records). The group is known for well organized protests including one that led to riots in Toledo, Ohio, in 2005. Demetrius Van Crocker, claimed to be a member of the NSM when he attempted to purchase C4 explosives and sarin nerve agent from an FBI agent in 2004, and was sentenced to thirty years in prison (45).

The American Nazi Party

Active: 1959-present **Leadership:** Martin Kerr and Rocky Suhayda **Aliases:** None. **Ideology:** Neo-Nazism, Neo-fascism, White nationalism, Antisemitism, White Supremacism and a Far-right political position.

Summary: The American Nazi Party (ANP) is a far-right American political party with its headquarters in Arlington VA. The support the views and beliefs of Adolf Hitler.

Operation Save America (OSA)

Active: 1988 – Present. **Leadership:** Founded as "Operation Rescue" by Randall Terry, current leader Rusty Thomas. **Aliases:** *Operation Rescue.* **Ideology:** Fundamentalist Christian conservative; anti-abortion, anti-Islam, and anti-homosexuality.

Summary: Operation Rescue was founded by Randell Terry to focus on protesting abortion clinics (46) but has since expanded to oppose Islam and homosexuality. The group primarily used protests and intimidation to block abortion clinics, placing them in the category of QT organization; however, in 1998, member James Kopp murdered an obstetrician, and in 2001, member

Jerry Reiter became an FBI informant and revealed that the group condones and teaches violent methods. They use violence to stop people who legally perform abortions in hopes that other health care professionals will change their ways, and that pushes this group beyond the QT category and squarely into the terrorist label.

Phineas Priesthood

Active: 1990 - Present. **Leadership:** None. **Aliases:** Phineas Priests (also spelled Phinehas). **Ideology:** Opposes interracial relationships, homosexuality, and abortion. It is a Christian group with anti-Semitic and anti-multiculturalism ideologies and they oppose taxation.

Summary: Based on the book, "Vigilantes of Christendom: The Story of the Phineas Priesthood" by White Supremacist, Richard Kelly Hoskins. The Phineas Priests members include anyone who acts out against (slays) the enemies of God, which apparently to include interracial couples, Jews, non-whites, and multiculturalists. The only known organized group that was associated with the Phineas Priesthood was 4 men who committed a series of robberies and bombings in 1990. Otherwise, the group associates only through their becoming Phineas Priests upon slaying their enemies. In 2014, Larry McQuilliams, who considered himself a "High Priest," shot up a police department, U.S. courthouse, and Mexican consulate in Texas.

Proud Boys

Active: 2016 - Present. **Leadership:** Gavin McInnes. **Aliases:** POYB **Ideology:** Self-proclaimed chauvinism and anti-white guilt; identified as a hate group by the SPLC for their rhetoric disparaging women, Muslims and other groups.

Summary: The Proud Boys became an all-male fraternity during the 2016 presidential elections. On their web site, they claim to be a group of western chauvinists who accept all races, religions, and sexual orientations, but they are often found rallying with other, known hate groups. The SPLC has documented the many racially charged actions and statements of the Proud Boy leader, Gavin McInnes. From the many video speeches by McInnes that can be found online, it is clear the he does not think he hates anyone. He simply believes that everyone has a place and anyone who does not have the same racial, physical, and ideological profile, has a place below him. That alone, however, does not make him or his organization terrorists. That fact that violence is expected wherever they gather, and that they have a paramilitary wing dedicated to protecting those who voice similar ideologies places them on the list of QT organizations.

Public Enemy Number 1 (PEN1)

Active: 1985 - Present. **Leadership:** Donald Reed "Popeye" Mazza. **Aliases:** PDS, PEN1, PEN1 Skins, PEN1 Death Squads, PENI. **Ideology:** White supremacy.

Summary: PEN1 has existed for more than 20 years and is one of the largest skinhead groups currently operating in the United States (47). It was formed in the 1980s by youths in the punk music scene. The group is involved in the drug trade and associated criminal activity. It does include female members, but they are typically in support roles only. PEN1 is affiliated with the Aryan Brotherhood and have a presence in the U.S. prison system. While most of their violence appears to be in support of the gang and its criminal activity, its expression of white supremacy gives its violence an ideological base, and so PEN1 is a QT organization.

Republic of New Africa (RNA)

Active: 1968 – present. **Leadership:** Founder, two brothers, Milton and Richard Henry. **Aliases:** sometimes spelled Afrika, New Africa. **Ideology:** Black separatism, they believed that an independent black republic should be formed within the southern United States, and the U.S. government should pay millions in reparations.

Summary: The Republic of New Africa is a Black Nationalist organization that was created in 1968 when a delegation of several hundred met in Detroit, Michigan, and adopted a declaration of independence (48). The members believed that an independent black republic should be created out of the southern United States, and they planned to establish that republic through armed resistance in the South and sabotage in the North (Ibid). The FBI determined that the RNA was seditious and raided several meetings, which led to the arrest and repeated imprisonment of RNA leaders (Ibid). From Exile in Cuba and then in China first president of the RNA, Robert Williams, called for the violent destruction of property, the white suppressors, and the U.S. government. Although the group has not been successful, its plan for using violence to further its goal of creating a new republic makes it a terrorist organization. Now less active and less known, it still claims to work toward a free republic within North America, holds annual meetings in Washington, D.C., and elects new representatives to the RNA government.

Revolutionary People's Group (RPG)

Active: 2012 **Leadership:** NA **Aliases:** NA **Ideology:** Anti-government and anti-corporate America

Summary: This group was an anarchist group which spawned from the non-violent Occupy Cleveland, an offshoot of the Occupy Wall Street Movement. Occupy sought to eliminate the inequities created by government policies that favored corporate America. The Revolutionary People's Group took that one step further, calling for anarchy. They recruited at Occupy events, hoping to find like-minded people, and so it is likely that they thought they were advancing the cause of Occupy.

Anthony Hayne, Brandon L. Baxter, Connor C. Stevens, Joshua S. Stafford, and David Wright made plans to destroy symbols of corporate America in the greater Cleveland area. They were arrested in 2012 when they purchased a fake bomb made to look like C4 that could be detonated from a cell phone. They planted it on the Route 82 Bridge and attempted to detonate it.

Sovereign Citizens Movement (SCM)

Active: 1980s – Present. **Leadership:** Regionally specific: Barton Albert Bates, Samuel Lynn Davis, Ronald Delorme, Nature El Bey, Roger Elvick, Kurt F. Johnson, Dale Scott Heineman, David Wynn Miller, Winston Shrout, James Timothy Turner, and Dr. Glenn Richard Unger. **Aliases:** *None.* **Ideology:** Right-wing anarchist ideology, antigovernment.

Summary: The sovereign citizens' movement was started in the 1980s as a White Supremacist and anti-Semitic group, but in 2000 the focus changed to strong antigovernment beliefs, and many of the current members are African American (49). The group supposes the existence of Sovereigns who are not under the jurisdiction of the U.S. government and therefore follow common law, thus choosing which laws to obey and which to ignore, and they think they can figure out the legal tactics necessary to proclaim themselves as Sovereigns (50). Sovereign Citizens refuse to acknowledge the authority of most government entities, including law enforcement and the IRS (Ibid). At first inspection, members of the movement appear to be criminals who respond violently when caught. They are a nuisance, filing confusing and consternating legal suits to harass the authorities who prosecute them. They are also killers, having killed police officers during traffic stops. The violence of Sovereign Citizens, however, is not always a direct response to law enforcement after being caught breaking the law. They also threaten and premeditate violent acts against U.S. government entities.

In 2011, the U.S. Marshal Service arrested militia leader and sovereign, Schaeffer Cox, in Alaska (51). The group had stockpiled weapons, like machine guns and silencers and explosive devices, and expected a raid on their facilities. They plotted to kill two law enforcement officials for every one of their militia members killed in the expected raid (Ibid).

In 1995, Timothy McVeigh detonated a truck bomb in front of the Alfred P. Murrah Federal Building in Oklahoma, killing 168 people and injuring almost 700 more (50). McVeigh was influenced by the National Alliance when he committed the atrocity that earned him a death sentence, but his accomplice, Terry Nichols, was a self-proclaimed sovereign citizen (Ibid).

Symbionese Liberation Army (SLA)

Active: 1973 – 1975. **Leadership:** Donald DeFreeze. **Aliases:** *None.* **Ideology:** The unity of all left-wing struggles; separatists.

Summary: In the mid-1970s, the Symbionese Liberation Army operated as a leftist revolutionary group in California (52). The word "symbionese" comes from "symbiosis," the biological term that identifies the interdependence of different species. The SLA believed there should be a union of classes and races (Ibid). Their leader, Donald DeFreeze, was an escaped convict and its initial seven members were prison activists. The SLA assassinated the first black superintendent of schools in Oakland, California, for supporting mandatory identification cards. They kidnapped Patty Hearst, who later joined the group and then claimed to be brainwashed by them and robbed several banks (Ibid). The group adopted the separatist idea of setting up sovereign entities within the U.S. Several members of the group were killed during a raid and the rest were eventually tracked down by the FBI. Several members served jail time and then resumed fairly mainstream lives except one who is serving a life sentence for the murder of the Oakland superintendent, and Hearst who was pardoned by President Clinton (Ibid).

United Freedom Front (UFF)

Active: 1970s – 1980s. **Leadership:** Raymond Luc Levasseur. **Aliases:** Sam Melville/Jonathan Jackson Unit, the Ohio 7. **Ideology:** Marxism.

Summary: The United Freedom Front was a Marxist group active in the 1970s and 1980s (53). Known formerly as the Sam Melville/Jonathan Jackson Unit, or the Ohio 7 (named after the 1984 arrest of UFF members in Ohio) the group was indicted with more than 20 bombings and nine bank robberies. The UFF was formed to protest the involvement of the U.S. in Central America (54).

Weather Underground Organization (WUO)

Active: 1969 – 1977. **Leadership:** Bill Ayres. **Aliases:** Weatherman, Weather Underground, and The Weathermen. **Ideology:** Militant radical left-wing to include Marxism–Leninism, communism, and anti-imperialism.

Summary: The WUO split off from the Students of the Democratic Society in 1969, seeking to spread communism through violent revolution (55). The name of the group came from Bob Dylan's "Subterranean Homesick Blues," in particular, the line *"You don't need a weatherman to know which way the wind blows."* The group was trying to convey its belief that global revolution was inevitable (Ibid). They are known for the "National Action" in 1969, which the newspapers called the "Days of Rage" when thousands of young people assaulted the police, whom they called, "pigs" (Ibid). They began bombing government targets in 1970, preceding each by a warning to prevent loss of life, and explaining each one afterward with a "weather report" (Ibid).

Chapter Two Summary

As stated at the beginning of the chapter, domestic terrorist organizations are a combination of groups committing terrorist acts for political, ideological and religious motives. The level of activity has waned for many and has become nonexistent for others. This chapter presented twenty-nine domestic terrorist organizations. Only five of them came into existence after 2001. Twenty-one of them started before 1995, and the oldest, The Klan, started in 1869. Nineteen of the groups presented in this chapter are still active, while ten have disappeared; there is a debate as to the Aryan Nation's activity.

The active groups focus on saving animals, the environment, hate of a particular race, or stopping abortions. Militant right and left-wing groups have dissipated, some of the leaders sought advanced degrees and involved themselves in politics. Cuban expatriates and Puerto Rican anti-colonialists are still vocal but not violent. Terrorist acts that include murder and destruction seldom inspire support from the general public, and so perhaps the now-defunct groups realized this and have changed their tactics. Maybe they found a voice on the internet and are pacified by being heard without shedding blood. The Jewish Defense League, for example, is still in operation, but only online.

Based on our definition of QT, many militias and hate groups that are not listed in this chapter are likely to fit into that category. The SPLC estimated that the number of hate groups in the U.S. reached 917 in 2016 (56). Many hate groups are just one act of violence away from becoming terrorists; but if the group's goal is simply to kill the target of their hate without using the fear generated from that violence to induce a change in policy or law, then it is still not a terrorist act. Many groups were considered for inclusion in this chapter, and because the number of violent groups is so large, some may have been overlooked. We feel, however, that the twenty-one domestic terrorist organizations and four QT organizations described here are highly representative and provide good examples of the terrorist groups that exist within the U.S. borders.

Chapter Three

Terror Cells in the United States

The terrorist cell is the smallest organizational unit of a terrorist organization. It can be as few as three individuals who come together to advance their common goal which is often the ideology of the larger organization. Many terrorist organizations use some form of cell strategy because the smaller group can act more inconspicuously, staying under the radar of law enforcement. There are three basic types of cells. The traditional cell is a small group that prepares to execute instructions from the larger organization. Self-starter cells act without much guidance from the larger organization. Sleeper cells maintain an inconspicuous lifestyle, preparing behind the scene so that when they are called upon by the larger organization they can act quickly. When a high number of convictions related to acts of terrorism occur in one location, it may be related to a terror cell (see Chapter 7, Is Your Neighbor a Terrorist). The following list identifies cells known to exist in the U.S. since 9/11, whose members have been arrested for acts related to terrorism.

Alaska SC Cell

The five members of this cell included Schaeffer Cox (leader), Lonnie and Karen Vernon, Coleman Barney and Michael Anderson. Their mission was to kill several Alaska State Troopers and U.S. District Court Judge Ralph Beistline, but their plot ended in 2011 when the group was arrested. According to Alaska State Troopers, the group stockpiled weapons and conducted surveillance on the homes of two troopers. They were aligned with the Sovereign Citizen Movement.

Boston Terror Cell

The three members of this cell included Usaama Abdullah Rahim, Nicholas Rovinski, and David Wright. Rahim was David's uncle and Nicholas was a friend. In 2015, Usamma died in a shoot-out with the police and FBI while brandishing a knife. The cell's original goal was to behead Pamela Geller, an outspoken anti-Muslim activist, but when that proved too difficult, they wanted to behead a police officer instead. They supported ISIS.

Columbus Terror Cell

Three members of this cell were convicted of terrorism-related crimes in 2003, but the actual number of members may be much higher. Two of the members, Iyman Faris and Christopher Paul, were American citizens. The third, Nuradin Abdi, was Somalian. It is suspected that Faris and his small group were a sleeper cell.

Faris and Paul plotted to bring down the Brooklyn Bridge. Faris traveled to Afghanistan to train, and while there he was introduced to Osama bin Laden.

D.C. Five / Pakistani Five Cell

Umar Farooq, Waqar Hassan Khan, Ahmed Abdullah Minni, Aman Hassan Yemer, and Ramy Zamzam, the leader, were members of the D.C. Five, also known as the Pakistani Five Cell. These five Muslim Americans from Virginia were arrested in 2009. They tried to find training to become jihadist guerrillas, planned to fight U.S. soldiers in Afghanistan, and may have been planning an attack in the United States. Khan had been convicted a year earlier for stealing packages from the UPS where he worked. Minni had a habit of watching and praising videos of attacks on the U.S. that he found on YouTube.

Florida Cell

Members of a south Florida-based cell included Mohammed Hesham Youssef, Kifah Jayyousi , Jose Padilla, Adham Amin Hassoun, and Kassem Daher. This terrorist support cell was designed to send money, physical assets, and mujahideen (warriors) recruits to overseas conflicts to fight violent jihad. The group had been monitored by the FBI for almost a decade before its members were arrested in 2001 and 2002.

Fort Dix plot / Fort Dix Five

The 2007 Fort Dix attack plot involved a group of five Muslim men. Three of the men were brothers: Dritan, Shain, and Eljvir Duka. One, Mohamad Shnewer, was a U.S. citizen and Eljvir's brother-in-law. The fifth, Serdar Tatar, was a friend. A sixth man, Agron Abdullahu was also involved. The men were found guilty of conspiring to stage an attack against U.S. Military personnel stationed at Fort Dix, New Jersey.

ISIS NY Cell

Fareed Mumuni, Munther Saleh, and Samuel Rahamin Topaz were arrested in different incidents in 2015. They plotted to bomb landmarks in New York and travel abroad to join ISIS. On one occasion, Mumini and Saleh charged at a federal agent with knives. Mumuni stabbed an FBI agent during execution of a search warrant. Saleh was trying to learn how to build a pressure-cooker bomb and allegedly received instruction from an ISIS official.

Jihadist Cell

Daniel Joseph Maldonado (Daniel Aljughaifi), Tarek Mehanna, and Ahmad Abousamra wanted to participate in violent jihad against American interests and to die on the battlefield. They provided material support to terrorists and attempted to radicalize others. They traveled to the Middle East in 2004 to train at terrorist training camps and prepare for armed jihad against U.S. interests and in support of establishing an independent Islamic State. Maldonado was captured in Somalia in 2007 and turned over to U.S. authorities. Mehanna was arrested in Texas and Abousamra was killed during an air strike in Syria.

Lackawanna Six / Buffalo Six Cell

Members included Muktar Al-Bakri, Sahim Alwan, Faysal Galab, Yahya Goba, Shafal Mosed, Yasein Taher, and a seventh member, Jaber Elbaneh. They were arrested for training at an al-Qaeda camp in Afghanistan in 2001. They admitted to hearing Osama Bin Laden speak about men ready to give their lives for the cause and were afraid to say anything after the 9/11 attack. Some of them claim to have talked to Bin Laden directly.

Elbaneh never returned to the U.S. and is assumed to be imprisoned in Yemen for crimes that he committed in country. The six who returned were suspected of being a sleeper cell. Al-Bakri was arrested in Bahrain in 2002 and was the first to admit that the group trained with al-Qaeda. The remaining members were arrested or convicted in 2003. Alwan was the first American to give a full interview of his experience at an al-Qaeda affiliated training camp.

Miami Seven / Liberty City Seven Cell

This terror cell may have been religious extremists and may have been supported by al-Qaeda. They were arrested in 2006 for plotting to attack the Sears Tower in Chicago and a federal building in Miami. Members included four American citizens, Burson Augustin, Rothschild Augustine, Narseal Batiste (the leader), and Stanley Grant Phanor; and three residents, Patrick Abraham, Naudimar Herrera, and Lyglenson Lemorin.

Newburgh Four

The members of the Newburgh Four cell included Onta Williams, Laguerre Payen, James Cromitie, and David Williams. They were arrested in 2009 when an FBI informant reported their plot to detonate explosives outside a Bronx synagogue and fire what they believed were stinger missile at National Guard planes at Stewart Air National Guard Base. They accused the FBI of entrapment; however, the U.S. Court of Appeals, Second Circuit, upheld the convictions and sentences based on a predisposition to engage in the criminal misconduct which was evident in conversations recorded by the informant.

NY Terror Cell

This cell was composed of four Americans, Mahud Faruq Brent, Abdulrahman Farhane, Tarik Shah, and Rene Wright (Rafiq Abdus Sabiur). They were arrested in 2005 for supporting terrorist organizations. Brent was trained at a terrorist training camp in Pakistan.

Raleigh Jihad Group / Quantico Attack

Daniel Boyd (leader), his sons Zakariya and Dylan Boyd, Anes Subasic, Mohammad Omar Aly Hassan, Ziyad Yaghi, and Hysen Sherifi were arrested in 2008 for planning to attack the U.S. Marine base at Quantico and targets overseas. Sherifi was also convicted of conspiracy to commit murder as he tried to have people killed who had testified against him. Jude Kenan Moammad fled to Pakistan when the group was arrested and was killed in 2011 in a drone strike that did not target him specifically.

Revolution Muslim (RM)

This cell started in 2007 in New York City and promoted forming a traditional Islamic state by overthrowing governments in Muslim-majority nations. They also wanted to end "Western imperialism." Its leaders were Jesse Curtis Morton, Joseph Cohen (Yousef Mohamid Al-Khattab), and Zachary Adam Chesser. In 2010, they tried to reorganize as a Muslim think tank named "Islam Policy," but by 2013 all three leaders were serving time in prison and the organization faded.

Texas Cartoon Terrorists

Three known members, Nadir Hamid Soofi, Elton Simpson, and Decarus Lowell Thomas, planned an attack on the Curtis

Culwell Center in Garland, Texas, in 2015. Infuriated by a cartoon exhibit featuring the Prophet Muhammad, Soofi and Simpson drove from Arizona to Texas, armed with assault rifles, handguns, and ammunition that they received from Thomas. They shot a security guard in the ankle but were killed before they reached the exhibit. The three discussed the attack at Thomas's home. This was the first attack on U.S. soil for which ISIS claimed responsibility. No connection has been proven, but Thomas was also accused of encouraging his friends to act in support of ISIS.

The Portland Seven Cell

The Portland Seven included Patrice Lumumba Ford, Jeffrey Leon Battle, October Martinique Lewis, Habis Abdulla al Saoub, Maher Hawash, Muhammad Ibrahim Bilal, and Ahmed Ibrahim Bilal. They were arrested in 2002 and 2003 for attempting to join al-Qaeda and the Taliban. Ahmed Bilal is the brother of Muhammad Ibrahim Bilal. Bilal turned himself into security officials at an Islamic university in Malaysia where he had been studying. He was deported back to the U.S.

Toledo Terror Cell

The Ohio-based group was mainly comprised of two U.S. citizens, Mohammad Zaki Amawi and Marwan Othman El-Hindi, and a permanent resident from Lebanon, Wassim Mazloum. They were arrested in 2006 for conspiring to commit terrorist acts against Americans overseas. Two cousins, Khaleel Ahmed and Zubair Ahmed were arrested in 2007, having been recruited and trained to take on the group's mission. Bilal Mazloum, brother of Wassim, was also arrested for providing false statements to the FBI during the investigation.

Virginia Jihad Cell

This North Virginia Cell included eleven men arrested for training at a jihadist training camp abroad and planning terrorist attacks. Six pleaded guilty, another three were convicted of making false statements to the FBI. The group allegedly used military-style paintball games for training. Members of this terror group included (the first three have U.S. Military experience) Allen Walter Iyon (Hammad Abdur-Raheem), Donald Surratt, Randall Blue Chapman (Seifullah), Ali al-Tamimi, Ali Asad Chandia, Khwaja Mahmood Hasan, Masoud Ahmad Khan, Randall Todd Royer, Sabri Benkahla, and Yong Ki Kwon.

Chapter Three Summary

This chapter presented information about 19 groups consider to be terror cells. In some cases, like the Revolutionary People's Group, the ties are with a socio-political group that was not a terror organization itself, but the cell recruited from the larger group and took its mission to an extreme. For some groups, their terror cell designation is more obvious because they supported or were supported by a known terrorist organization.

These twenty-two terrorist cells were dismantled thanks to law enforcement authorities. Unfortunately, we often do not know about terror cells until the authorities infiltrate and arrest them. If we know the typical characteristics of people who are recruited, and become terrorists, perhaps more cells can be discovered and dismantled before they act. Better still, perhaps we can intervene in a way that prevents radicalization so that no cell is created, and no jail time is necessary.

Chapter Four

International Terrorist Organizations

Terrorism is not a 9/11 phenomenon. One of the first international terrorist organizations was the Sicarii, a group of Jewish zealots founded in the first century AD with the goal of overthrowing the Romans (57). The Second World War brought about modern terrorism with the rise of nationalist movements. To date the al-Qaeda terrorist organization has done more damage to the United States than any other terror organization, foreign or domestic.

U.S. Citizens have become aligned with or pledged their allegiance to at least eighteen different international terrorist organizations. As expected, the most familiar groups, al-Qaeda (AQ) and Islamic State of Iraq and Syria (ISIS) had the most allegiances (Figure 1).

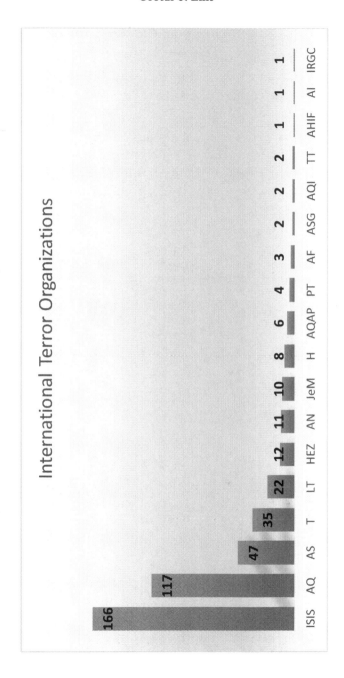

International Terror Organizations

ISIS	AQ	AS	T	LT	HEZ	AN	JeM	H	AQAP	PT	AF	ASG	AQI	TT	AHIF	AI	IRGC
166	117	47	35	22	12	11	10	8	6	4	3	2	2	2	1	1	1

Figure 1:The number of American terrorists who aligned with each of the following international terrorist organizations: Al Fuqra (AF); Al Haramain Islamic Foundation (AHIF); Ansar al-Islam (AI); Nusra Front or Jabhat al-Nusra (AN); Al-Qaeda (AQ); Al-Qaida in the Arabian Peninsula (AQAP); Al-Qaeda in Iraq (AQI); Al-Shabaab (AS); Hamas (H); Hezbollah (Hez); Iranian Islamic Revolutionary Guard Corps (IRGC); Islamic State of Iraq and Syria (ISIS/ISIL); Jaish-e-Mohammed (JeM); Lashkar-e-Tayyiba (LT); Pakistan Taliban (PT); Taliban (T); and the Tamil Tigers (TT).

Allegiances also went to Pakistan Taliban (PT), Jaish-e-Mohammed (JeM), and Lashkar-e-Tayyiba (LT) in Pakistan. In Iraq, Americans were aligned with al-Qaeda in Iraq (AQI) and Ansar al-Islam (AI). Some were affiliated with Nusra Front or Jabhat al-Nusra (AN) in Syria, Taliban (T) in Afghanistan, al-Shabaab (AS) in Somalia, Iranian Islamic Revolutionary Guard Corps (IRGC) in Iran, Hezbollah (Hez) in Lebanon, and Hamas (H) in the Palestinian region.

Connections were found to al-Qaeda in the Arabian Peninsula (AQAP), Al Haramain Islamic Foundation (AHIF) based in Saudi Arabia but with branches all over the world, Al Fuqra (AF) which operates on several continents, Tamil Tigers (TT) in Eastern Shri Lanka, and Abu Sayyaf Group (ASG) in the Philippines. The number of Americans that have aligned with each group is shown in Figure 1 and descriptions of the organizations follow.

Abu Sayyaf Group (ASG)

Active: 1991 - Present. **Leadership:** Abdurajak Abubakar Janjalani (founder). **Estimated Size:** 400 **Ideology:** Islamist, Jihadist, Salafi, Wahhabi.

Summary: The name Abu Sayyaf means, "Father of Swordsmen." This Islamic group started in 1991 with the goal of establishing an independent Islamic state in the Southern Philippines. Al-Qaeda provided financial help to start the group. Philippine government forces killed the founder in 1998 and the succeeding faction leaders in 2006 and 2007, leaving the organization in small, squabbling factions. Some have pledged loyalty to ISIS and others remaining committed to establishing a local caliphate. Abu Sayyaf is known for raising money by kidnapping innocents and beheading them if the ransom is not paid.

Al Fuqra (AF) / Jamaat ul-Fuqraa

Active: 1980 – Present. **Leadership:** Sheikh Mubarik Ali Jilani Hashemi. **Estimated Size:** 3000 **Ideology:** Muslim Extremist.

Summary: Jamaat ul-Fuqraa means the Community of the Impoverished. The group mainly operates in Canada and the United States, but is present in Pakistan, the Caribbean, Europe, and the Ivory Coast. Operating two front groups, Muslims of the Americas and Quranic Open University, the members choose to terrorize with murders and fire-bombings and considers the United States an enemy. Traci Elaine Upshur and her husband Vincente Rafael Pierre (Rafael Upshur) are two U.S. citizens aligned with this group.

Al Haramain Islamic Foundation (AHIF)

Active: 1988 – 2004. **Leadership:** Aqeel Abdulaziz Aqeel al-Aqeel. **Estimated Size:** Unknown **Ideology:** Muslim NGO.

Summary: Al-Haramain Islamic Foundation (AHIF) was a charity foundation, based in Saudi Arabia. The foundation used most of their funds to feed poor Muslims around the world, a small amount went to al-Qaeda, but that money was "a major source of funds" for the terrorist group. Branches of the charity around the world have been designated as terrorist organizations. In September 2004, a U.S. Department of the Treasury investigation claimed to have found "direct links" between the U.S. branch of the foundation and Osama bin Laden. Pete Seda (Pirouz Sedaghaty), a naturalized U.S. citizen from Iran, was the leader of the AHIF chapter in the U.S. He avoided arrest by living in Iran and Syria for five years. When he returned to the U.S. in 2008, he was arrested and in 2010 he was convicted of sending money in support of Islamic fighters in Chechnya. The conviction was overturned in 2013, and the charity entered a plea deal in 2014 that involved dropping the charges against Seda.

Al-Qaeda (AQ)

Active: 1988 – present. **Leadership:** Ayman Mohammed Rabie al-Zawahiri. **Estimated Size:** as of 2009 AQ had approximately 200-300 commanders **Ideology:** Wahhabism, Salafist jihadism, Qutbism, Pan-Islamism, Anti-Communism, Anti-Zionism, and Antisemitism.

Summary: Al-Qaeda is a terrorist organization founded by Osama bin Laden. The FBI gave them the name because "al-Qaeda" means "the base," and that is what bin Laden and his followers called the area where they trained (58). Osama bin Laden is the most recognized name in Muslim extremism, but he certainly did not start fanaticism in the Middle East (58). Nor did his death in 2011 bring an end to the jihadist warrior, the mujahideen (59).

More than half of the American citizens that have aligned themselves with international terrorist organizations have chosen al-Qaeda. It has spread throughout the Middle East and Africa and has planted roots in the U.S. It seems to be less of a threat today than it was just a few years ago, especially since the rise of another organization, ISIS, in 2014 (60). Al-Qaeda is still active, though, and individuals still proclaim their alliance with it. The headquarters is in Pakistan, but they have affiliated organizations around the world.

The purpose of al-Qaeda was to bring together and train jihadists from all over the world, and then send them back to their home countries where they could take steps to overthrow the local government. By overthrowing un-Islamic governments, they could form a new global caliphate. Al-Qaida focused their attacks on the "far enemy," the United States, and other Western countries.

The American terrorists who are aligned with al-Qaeda resided in eighteen different U.S. states. The majority were from New York, Ohio and Florida. The local numbers may be inflated due to Terror Cells. Ohio, for example, was home to two Terror Cells, one in Toledo and another in Columbus. Other notable locations with al-Qaeda aligned terror cells are Portland, Oregon; Miami, Florida; Washington, D.C.; and New York City.

Nidal Hasan killed thirteen people and injured another thirty-two in 2009 at Fort Hood, Texas. Hasan had corresponded with Anwar al-Awlaki, an American al-Qaeda leader. Hasan was a major in the U.S. Army Medical Corps, was college educated, unmarried, and thirty-eight years old. He was sentenced to death in 2013 (61).

American citizens have also been aligned with two al-Qaeda affiliated organizations: al-Qaeda in the Arabian Peninsula (AQAP) and al-Qaeda in Iraq (AQI).

Al-Qaida in the Arabian Peninsula (AQAP)

Active: 2009 – present. **Leadership:** Abu Musab al-Zarqawi (KIA), Abu Ayyub al-Masri (KIA). **Estimated Size:** as of 2009 AQAP had approximately 6000-7000 members. **Ideology:** Salafism, Salafist jihadism, Anti-Zionism, Antisemitism

Summary: The AQAP is based in Yemen. U.S. citizens who claim to be aligned with AQAP, include Justin Kaliebe, Samir Zafar Khan, Marcos Alonso Zea, Mohamed Bailor Jalloh, Barry

Walter Bujol, Nidal Hasan, and Carlos Leon Bledsoe. One was killed in a U.S. drone strike, two received life sentences, and one is still at large. Anwar al-Awlaki, an American citizen and al-Qaeda leader, influenced four of them. Their ages range from twenty-four to thirty-eight. One successful attack inspired by AQAP happened in 2009 in Little Rock, Arkansas. Abdulhakim Mujahid Muhammad, born Carlos Leon Bledsoe from Tennessee, opened fire on a U.S. military recruiting station, drive-by style. Private William Long was killed, and Private Quinton Ezeagwula was wounded.

Al-Qaeda in Iraq (AQI)

Active: 2004 – present. **Leadership:** Ayman Mohammed Rabie al-Zawahiri. **Estimated Size:** Unknown. **Ideology:** Like other AQ organizations.

Summary: When al-Zarqawi originally came onto the scene he positioned himself as a rival to bin Laden, but in 2004 he officially declared allegiance to al-Qaeda, changing the name of his organization from Unification and Jihad to al-Qaeda in Iraq. They fought in opposition to the Shi'ite-dominated government brought about by the U.S. occupation of Iraq. In 2006, they split from al-Qaeda and became the Islamic State of Iraq. Abdifatah Aden was a follower of AQI.

Al-Shabaab (AS)

Active: 2006 – present. **Leadership:** Ahmad Umar (Abu Ubaidah). **Estimated Size:** approximately 7000-9000 members. **Ideology:** Salafist jihadism, Anti-Zionism, Antisemitism, Wahhabism.

Summary: Al-Shabaab means "The Youth." Several U.S. citizens are aligned with AS, and many of the parents came from Somalia, where al-Shabaab fights to oust the government. Their ages ranged from twenty to thirty years old. Two of the men remain at large while another was a suicide bomber. In 2011, Farah Mohamed Beledi killed himself using a vehicle born improvised explosive device (VBIED) in an attack in Somalia. American citizen, Omar Shafik Hammami, (Abu Mansoor al-Amriki), was a leader in al-Shabaab. In 2012 Hammami was added to the FBI's Most Wanted Terrorists list.

Ansar al-Islam (AI)

Active: 2000 – present. **Leadership:** Abu Ahmad. **Estimated Size:** Hundreds. **Ideology:** Salafism, Salafist Jihadism, Wahhabism.

Summary: Based in Iraqi Kurdistan, the mission of this terror group is to overthrow the government of Iraq, remove all foreign militaries from Iraq, institute Shariah Law, and set up a Sunni Islamist state in Iraq. Mohammed Mosharref Hossain had been in contact with AI several times between 1999 and 2001, and connections were also evident in 2003, prompting the FBI to investigate him. In 2006, he was arrested in a sting operation. Hossain tried to launder money related to terrorist support.

Hamas (H)

Active: 1987 – present. **Leadership:** Khaled Meshaal. **Estimated Size:** Unknown. **Ideology:** Palestinian nationalism, Sunni Islamism, Islamic nationalism, Islamic fundamentalism, Anti-Zionism, Antisemitism.

Summary: During the beginning of the first Palestinian uprising, Hamas was formed, derived from the Palestinian branch of the Muslim Brotherhood. The group's goal is to establish an Islamic Palestinian state in historic Palistine. "Hamas" is actually an acronym of Harakat al-Muqawamah al-Islamiyyah, which means "Islamic Resistance Movement." Hamas is concentrated in the Gaza Strip and areas of the West Bank. The Izz al-Din al-Qassam Brigade (EQB) is the military branch of Hamas and has been responsible for many anti-Israel attacks in both Israel and Palestine.

In 2010 Theophilus Burroughs, an American citizen, ex-Marine, and high school music teacher was arrested for dealing military-grade weapons to agents who he thought were Hamas. The Bronx teacher suggested the agents attack a Jewish center or police precinct. He was convicted in 2015.

In 2004, the Holy Land Foundation, the largest Muslim charity in America, was shut down for providing funds to Hamas. Its five leaders were jailed. Two of them, Abdulraham Odeh and Ghassan Elashi were U.S. citizens.

Hezbollah (HEZ)

Active: 1982 – present. **Leadership:** Hassan Nasrallah. **Estimated Size:** 20,000 to 50,000. **Ideology:** Islamic nationalism, Anti-Zionism, Anti-Western imperialism, Shia Jihadism, Khomeinism, Anti-West, Anti-Semitism.

Summary: Hezbollah is literally translated, "Party of Allah." It is a Shi'ite, Muslim political party based in Lebanon. They are also a militant group, labeled a terrorist organization by the United States and the European Union. It was formed in response to the Israeli invasion of Lebanon. Hezbollah has been responsible for several anti-U.S. terrorist attacks.

Several American citizens have been imprisoned for providing or attempting to provide material support to Hezbollah. Those convicted include Said Mohamad Harb, a North Carolina man sent to prison in 2002, Hor and Amera Akl, an Ohio couple, and Khaled T. Safadi, a Florida man, who were caught in separate incidents in 2010.

Iranian Islamic Revolutionary Guard Corps (IRGC)

Active: 1982 – present. **Leadership:** Ayatollah Khamenei. **Estimated Size:** 120,000–125,000. **Ideology:** Khomeinism, Anti-Imperialism, Shia Islamism, Anti-Zionism, Antisemitism.

Summary: Founded after the 1979, Islamic revolution in Iran, with the responsibility of defending the revolution, the IRGC was created as a "people's army" similar to the U.S. National Guard. Today, it presides over a vast power structure, with influence over almost every aspect of Iranian life. It promotes the Islamic Revolution ideal worldwide.

Mansour Arbabsiar is a naturalized American citizen who sold used cars in Texas. His cousin was a high-ranking official in the Quds Force, a special operations unit of the IRGC. For the IRGC, Arbabsiar planned to hire a Mexican drug cartel to blow up a restaurant in Washington, D.C., in order to assassinate the Saudi Ambassador. The U.S. Drug Enforcement Agency (DEA) intercepted his plans and posed as agents for the cartel. Arbabsiar was arrested in 2011 as he tried to finalize the assassination plot.

Islamic State of Iraq and Syria (ISIS) / Islamic State of Iraq and the Levant

Active: 1999 – present. **Leadership:** Abu Bakr al-Baghdadi. **Estimated Size:** Unknown. **Ideology:** Salafism, Salafist Jihadism, Wahhabism.

Summary: This organization was known as Al-Qaida in Iraq in 2003 and became the Islamic State of Iraq (ISI) in 2006. When they expanded into Syria in 2013, they became the Islamic State of Iraq and Syria (ISIS). Their goal, however, was to set up a broader Islamic state to include Syria, Lebanon, Israel, Jordon, and the region of Palestine, an area called the Levant, and so several world leaders began to call them Islamic State of Iraq and the Levant (ISIL). ISIL is a violent jihadist organization. They rule with brutality, carrying out public executions, beheadings, crucifixions, and actively encouraged the rape of women and girls. They recruit Muslims from around the world and invest heavily in marketing and media. Non-Sunni Muslims are also forced to convert, leave, or be killed. Sunni Muslims that do not agree with ISIL's interpretation of Islam are punished harshly or killed.

ISIS has inspired more than a few American citizens to lend support or to commit acts of terror in its name. Many of them were born in the U.S. and some were naturalized citizens. The inspired tried to join ISIS to fight in the Middle East. Amiir Farouk Ibrahim was born in Pennsylvania and lived with his parents in Saudi Arabia and Egypt before returning to the U.S. for college. In 2013, his passport was found in Syria. He had been killed while fighting for ISIS.

Edward Archer shot a West Philadelphia police officer sitting in his cruiser in 2016. Archer told officers that he did it because of his allegiance to the Islamic State.

Keonna Thomas spent two years promoting ISIS online before she was arrested in 2015. She married an ISIS fighter through Skype and planned to meet with him in Syria. She even voiced her desire to take part in a suicide attack.

Jabhat al-Nusra (AN)/ Nusra Front

Active: 2012 – present. **Leadership:** Abu Mohammad al-Julani. **Estimated Size:** 10,000-20,000. **Ideology:** Salafism, Salafist Jihadism, Wahhabism.

Summary: The Nusra Front started as al-Qaeda's branch in Syria in 2011, when the leader of AQI sent military leaders into Syria to take advantage of the Syrian civil war and institute Sharia law. The leader, Abu Mohammad al-Julani, officially announced the new name, al-Nusra Front for the People of Al-Sham, in 2012. The Nusra Front, or Jabhat al-Nusra, was focused on overthrowing the Syrian government by attacking the Syrian military and conducting terrorist attacks on civilians in Syria. In 2016, al-Julani formally declared that it was cutting ties with al-Qaeda and renaming the organization to Jabhat Fateh al-Sham. It was renamed again in 2017 to Hayyat Tahrir al-Sham (HTS), the Organization for the Liberation of the Levant.

Abdifatah Aden (Abu Hassan al-Somali) was a naturalized U.S. citizen from Somalia who lived in Columbus, Ohio. In 2012, he posted videos and quotes by Anwar al-Awlaki online. He traveled to Syria in 2013 and died fighting for Nusra Front in 2014. His half-brother, Abdirahman Sheik Mohamud, traveled to Syria in 2014 to give Aden money and trained in an al-Nusra camp. Four days after his brother's death, he returned to the U.S. with plans to carry out terrorist attacks. He was arrested in 2015.

In 2013, Nicole Mansfield became the first American woman to be killed in Syria. She allegedly threw a grenade at Syrian government forces from her car. She and two other occupants were killed when the troops opened fire. She was a high-school dropout from Michigan, who earned a GED, attended community college, was briefly married to an Arab immigrant, and lived with a Muslim family before traveling to Syria. The Syrian military said she was part of the Nusra Front.

Jaish-e-Mohammed (JeM)

Active: 2000 – present. **Leadership:** Masood Azhar. **Estimated Size:** Several thousand followers. **Ideology:** Islamic fundamentalism.

Summary: This extremist Islamist group, based in Pakistan, aims to undermine Indian control of the Islamic Administered Kashmir (IAK). They want to unite the province with Pakistan under their interpretation of Shariah Law. Members of JeM kidnapped and beheaded the American journalist, Daniel Pearl. In addition to his connection to Ansar al-Islam, one of Mohammed Mosharref Hossain's twenty-seven convictions was trying to provide material support to JeM.

Lashkar-e-Tayyiba (LT)

Active: 1987 – present. **Leadership:** Hafiz Muhammad Saeed. **Estimated Size:** Several Thousand. **Ideology:** Ahl al-Hadith (Salafi).

Summary: Based in Pakistan, Lashkar-e-Tayyiba (Army of the Righteous) (Lashlar-e-Taiba) is one of the largest and most proficient of the Kashmir-focused militant groups. Their ultimate goal is to eliminate Indian power and create an Islamic caliphate in the Indian subcontinent. LT began as the military wing of Markaz-ud-Dawa-wal-Irshad, a Pakistani Islamist organization, in the early 1990s, and fought against the Soviets in Afghanistan before focusing on the Kashmir region. The Pakistani Inter-Service Intelligence (ISI) is suspected of supporting LT.

Several American citizens have aligned with LT. Most of them, including 3 with U.S. military experience, were members of the same terrorist cell, the Virginia Jihad Cell. David Headley (Daood Sayed Gilani), had a Pakistani father and American mother and lived in Chicago when he was arrested for helping to plan an attack on the Danish national newspaper for printing a cartoon image of the Prophet Mohammed. He also attended LT-sponsored terrorist training camps in Pakistan and worked with LT to plan attacks in Mumbai.

Taliban (T)

Active: 1994 – present. **Leadership:** Mawlawi Hibatullah Akhundzada. **Estimated Size:** 60,000. **Ideology:** Deobandi fundamentalism, Pashtunwali, Religious nationalism.

Summary: Taliban means "The Students." When the Soviet-Afghanistan war ended, Afghanistan was in chaos, and a group of Pashtun-Afghan students helped to end the fighting and restore order. The Taliban ruled in Afghanistan by force until 2001 using a strict interpretation of Islamic law (Shariah) with Pashtun tribal codes (Pashtunwali). The Taliban fled to Pakistan after the U.S. and the Northern Alliance removed them from power. The Taliban is fighting for a Pashtun-Afghan run Afghanistan with all foreign forces removed from the country. Their fight is not for dominance in the world, but for the country of Afghanistan.

Several of the U.S. citizens that aligned with the Taliban were also aligned with al-Qaeda. The majority of them were second, third or forth generation Americans. The remaining were citizens with Pakistani and Yemen heritage. The Lackawanna Six Cell, a group of Yemeni-Americans in New York, was loyal to the Taliban and Al-Qaeda.

Pakistan Taliban (PT) / Tehrik-e-Taliban

Active: 2007 – present. **Leadership:** Mufti Noor Wali Mehsud. **Estimated Size:** 25,000 in 2014. **Ideology:** Deobandi fundamentalism.

Summary: A Taliban affiliate, the Tehrik-e-Taliban is an alliance of militant networks formed in 2007 to unify opposition against the Pakistani military. Faisal Shahzad, a Pakistani-American naturalized citizen, trained with PT in Pakistan. He tried to use a car bomb in New York City's Times Square in 2010, but it failed to detonate. He was arrested while boarding a plane to Dubai.

Tamil Tigers / Liberation Tigers of Tamil Eelam

Active: 1976–2009. **Leadership:** Velupillai Prabhakaran (KIA). **Estimated Size: Inactive.** **Ideology:** Tamil nationalism, Separatism, Revolutionary socialism, Secularism

Summary: The Tamil Tigers is a guerrilla organization that sought to establish an independent Tamil state in eastern Sri Lanka. Established in 1976, Tamil Tigers quickly became one of the most sophisticated and tightly organized insurgent groups in the world. It is credited with over 200 suicide bombings and several political assassinations, including government officials and a former Prime Minister of India. The separatists were defeated in 2009 after a major military offensive that killed many of the fighters and the Tamil Tiger leadership.

The group relied on expatriates for support and set up branches around the world. The leader of operations in the U.S. was a Tamil-American, naturalized citizen, Karunakaran Kadasamy (Kauna). He oversaw the raising and transfer of millions of dollars, technology, and military grade weaponry.

He pled guilty in 2009 of providing material support and served five years of his twenty-year sentence before convincing the court that he believed he was providing humanitarian support to the Tamili people.

Chapter Four Summary

This chapter presented eighteen international terror organizations with which American terrorists were aligned. It is not a comprehensive list of international terror organizations. Recognized terror organizations like Boko Haram and FARC were not included because to date there have not been any Americans citizens convicted of joining or supporting them. The top three international terror groups that were successful in recruiting American citizens were the Islamic State of Iraq and the Levant (ISIS/ISIL), al-Qaeda (AQ), and al-Shabaab (AS). The leadership of the terror organizations are rarely aware that the Americans aligned with their group. Many, in fact, may only have been aligned in their own minds, but the intimacy of the connection is not as important as the reality that these men and women lent, or tried to lend their support, risking their lives, and/or the lives of others.

Humans are cultural, societal beings. One situation that make people ripe for recruitment into extremist organizations is when they feel isolated, alone, or displaced. It is our duty as family members, educators, and colleagues to help those with a desperate need to belong, to choose wise alliances that promote unity, respect, and acceptance instead of hate, racism, or dissidence.

Chapter Five

Education, Profession, and Marital Status

Now that we have defined terrorism and introduced the domestic and international terrorist groups, we will start to examine the demographic of the American terrorists. In order to understand the people who became terrorists, we will first bring to light their education, profession, and marital status.

Education

A positive correlation between advanced education and participation in terror groups has already been reported by others (62,63). We postulate one possible explanation for the high number of educated terrorists: frustration. The expectations associated with certain achievements may hold more weight in a person's mind than the actual achievements. If one spends the money and puts in the time to get an advanced education, for example, they expect positive reciprocity such as a well-paying job. If the job is not forthcoming, or the pay is less than desired, some people project blame onto the economy, community leaders, or the government. They become frustrated and more responsive to suggestions to act against those responsible, such as the leaders, government, and others, to courage equality. If a terrorist recruiter finds them in that frame of mind, they may be easily radicalized.

Some have suggested that providing education will help reduce recruitment into terror organizations and that the type of education (religious versus secular) is an important factor, while others refute that and point out that recruiting well-educated individuals would make interaction easier with educated targets (64,65). Marc Sageman, forensic psychiatrist and counter-terrorism consultant, found that most of the terrorists he interviewed had advanced studies in technology and the sciences (66). The level of education is unlikely to drive recruitment. Instead, susceptibility to recruitment is driven by an attitude of dissatisfaction and potential hostility derived from a sense of entitlement, and the perceived injustice or oppression that prevents them from achieving what their education should provide.

Organizations, such as al-Qaeda and ISIS, can be selective when choosing who to train and let into the fold. Education, it seems, would create a smarter, more dedicated, deadlier warrior. It is not surprising, therefore, that sixty percent of the terrorists in this study were college-educated. Of those with college experience, sixty-seven percent chose STEM (Science, Technology,

Engineering and Math) degrees (see Table 2), with several holding advanced or terminal degrees.

There were more students who committed acts of terrorism than any of the professions named in the next section. This is interesting because college life is often the first-time individuals experience freedom and begin to think for themselves. They form their own ideology and political and religious views instead of following those of their parents. If terrorist recruiters target that impressionable population, they have a better chance of biasing their ideologies at a relatively young age.

When the college majors and their relationships to STEM are categorized interesting patterns emerge, such as the popularity of STEM majors, and the expertise that the individuals take back to their terror organizations. Recruiting terrorists with the specializations identified below can be an accomplishment for the organization, and quite devastating if they were able to use them against the U.S.

College Majors of American Terrorists

Degree	Number of Terrorists	Field
Engineering	11	STEM
Computer science	8	STEM
Criminal justice	4	Not STEM
Nursing	4	STEM
Psychology	4	STEM
Biology	3	STEM
Business	3	Not STEM
Business administration	3	Not STEM
Economics	3	Not STEM
Education	3	Not STEM

Medical	3	STEM
Aeronautics	2	STEM
Chemistry	2	STEM
Chinese	2	Not STEM
Dental	2	STEM
History	2	Not STEM
Medical Degree (MD)	3	STEM
Pharmacy	2	STEM
Accounting	1	Not STEM
Fire science	1	STEM
Funeral services	1	STEM
Mass communications	1	Not STEM
Math	1	STEM
MBA	1	Not STEM
Multimedia	1	Not STEM
Philosophy	1	Not STEM
Physics	1	STEM
Political science	1	Not STEM
Premed	1	STEM
Radiology	1	STEM
Religious studies	1	Not STEM
Social worker/ Aeronautics	1	Not STEM
Sociology and Criminal Justice	1	Not STEM

Table 2: American Terrorists and Their Majors (inc. Science, Technology, Engineering and Math, STEM)

Profession

The occupational information was available for 235 American terrorists, and the top fourteen fields are listed in Table 3. Eight percent of the 235 terrorists were reported to be unemployed, and as already stated, more terrorists were students (sixteen percent) than any occupation. The most reported livelihood was general retail, but some of those included store owners, like Mufid Elfgeeh, who attempted to provide support to ISIS, sought to kill U.S. veterans, and owned a pizza shop in Rochester, New York. Several of the careers held by American terrorists would place them in strategic places or provide the tools for causing great harm or destruction or inducing panic.

Those in food service and health care might find their position convenient for exposing many people to harmful agents and inducing fear in those industries. The security industry, military, and martial arts may provide the training necessary to maximize damage and avoid capture. Computer, communications, and financial professionals can gain access to resources or harmful information, spread propaganda, or hinder economic assets.

Those in transportation could use their vehicle as a weapon. In fact, truck drivers control a weapon that weighs in excess of five U.S. tons, or nine thousand kilograms. Some of the American terrorists (nearly two percent, or four out of 235) were in the aviation industry. One of them, avionics technician Terry Loewen, born in the U.S., tried to blow up a truck full of explosives on the airport tarmac in Wichita, KS.

In all, the jobs could be categorized into thirty-two different fields of occupation, twelve of them only having one or two terrorists in them. The general distribution of professions among American terrorists is similar to the general public. One of the most informative statistics in this study are that sixteen percent of the identified terrorists were students and eight percent were unemployed. The unemployment rate in the U.S. was less than eight percent until just before 2009, between eight and ten percent between 2009 and 2012, and less than eight percent 2012 - 2018 (67). Although about one-third of the American terrorists were arrested during each of those periods, only fourteen percent of the unemployed terrorists were arrested during the period of greatest unemployment, between 2009 and 2012. The other eighty-six percent of unemployed terrorists were arrested when the general unemployment rate was below eight percent, signifying that they were still unemployed when the general rate of unemployment was low, and thus suggesting a connection between unemployment and recruitment into terrorism.

The statistics suggest that the populations most vulnerable to radicalization are the impressionable students and those frustrated by unemployment. When we consider that the majority of the American terrorists (sixty percent) were college educated, and the top two occupations were retail and miscellaneous labor, there may also be a large number of them crushed by under-employment; in other words, they were not gainfully employed in their degree field.

The Top Terrorist Industries

Retail	9%
Miscellaneous Labor	6%
Food Service	6%
Security Industry	6%
Health Care	6%
Transportation	4%
Computer/IT	4%
Military	4%
Teaching	3%
Construction	3%

Fitness/Martial Arts	3%
Communications	3%
Trucking	2%
Financial Industry	2%

Table 3: The Percent of Terrorists in The Top Fourteen Industries.

Marital Status

There are more single, male, American terrorists than married ones. Marital status is more difficult to assess than many of the other parameters because it is not standard to list marital status in court documents or law enforcement reports. Accessory documents, such as character witness letters, may reference relatives, but to determine status, we search news media reports. Local media tend to humanize individuals, and terrorists are no exception. It seems that if family exists, the new media will track them down for a statement. In some cases, single status was specifically stated, but if we were unable to find any mention of marital status after an extensive search, we assumed single status.

Ninety percent of males, and eighty-eight percent of females charged with acts of terror were age twenty or older at the time of their arrest. This would lead you to presume that more of them would be married. The majority, seventy-eight percent were not married (see Table 4). In fact, of the male terrorists, only sixteen percent were married (see Figure 2), but seventy percent of the females charged with acts of terror were married (see Figure 3). Similarly, while only nine percent of the males had children, twenty-one percent of the females were mothers.

Based on the large percentage of men who are single and low percentage with children, one might conclude that men with

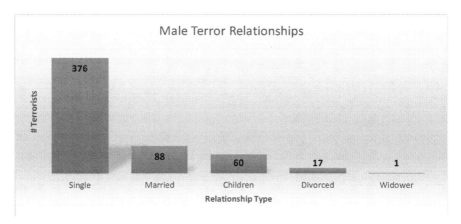

Figure 2: The number of male American terrorists in each relationship status indicated (N=483). For this study, all males not identified as married, divorced, or widowed were assumed to be single.

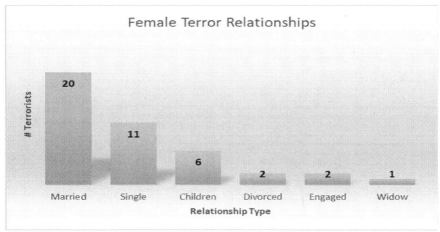

Figure 3: The number of female American terrorists in each relationship status indicated (N=36). For this study, all females not identified as married, divorced, engaged or widowed were assumed to be single.

family responsibilities are less likely to be radicalized. Perhaps they feel accountable for the survival and upkeep of their families and cannot be bothered with radical ideologies. Alternatively, American men that are more susceptible to radicalization may be less appealing to women. A more noteworthy conclusion could be drawn if we knew whether they married before or after radicalization.

American Terrorist Relationships

Status	Number of Terrorists	Percentage
Single	388	75%
Married	108	21%
Divorced	19	4%
Widowed	2	< 1%
Engaged	2	< 1%
Children	53	10%

Table 4: The Relationship Status of U.S. Citizens Charged with Acts Related to Terrorism Since 9/11

The females in this study have a relatively high rate of marriage and greater percentage with children. They represent less than ten percent of the total number of American terrorists, but more than forty percent of the married terrorists. Could it simply be that women are more family-centered? Half of the married, female terrorists were married to terrorists; another thirty-seven percent of them were convicted of acts related to terrorism with their husbands, or ex-husband in the case of October Martinique Lewis of the Portland Seven Cell. The women who become terrorists appear to be drawn to like-minded partners, or to the demographic with potential to become radicalized. In addition, based on the statistics it would appear that women seem not to let marriage stop them acting on their beliefs even if that leads them down a path of murder and death.

Half of the married, female terrorists were married to males also fitting the terrorist profile (see Figure 3). Two female terrorists were engaged to terrorists, and one more was divorced from a terrorist. One third of married, female terrorists kept their terrorist activities a secret from their spouses. When all of the data is presented one can posit that married women identified as terrorists are likely to recruit their husbands. On the other hand, it may be that women are more likely to become terrorists if their husband, or significant other, is a terrorist. Conversely, it seems that married men with law-aiding wives are not likely to get involved in terrorism, or crimes related to terrorism.

Chapter Five Summary

This chapter revealed that the majority of American citizens charges with acts related to terrorism have some college education, and more than sixty percent of them chose majors in STEM fields. Sixteen percent of the terrorists were students and eight percent were unemployed. General retail, miscellaneous labor, and workers in the food industry were among the most common jobs, suggesting that while the American terrorists were well educated, the jobs they held may not have been in their chosen career field. Jobs in the security and healthcare industries were common, and they have the potential to cause more damage or produce greater fear than other professions.

The American terrorists came from all economic classes. We also established that most male, American terrorists were single, but the opposite was true for females. The women convicted of crimes related to terrorism often bring along their husband or boyfriend when committing acts of terror.

Chapter Six

Mindset of a Terrorist

Nasra Hassan, an international relief worker from Pakistan, interviewed 250 Hamas militants in an effort to understand why young men become suicide bombers (68). Hassan found that the young men were sane and educated, not depressed or poor. Two of the militants were the progeny of millionaires who, she discovered, joined to fight for their fellow compatriots that were less financially well off. Additionally, Hassan discovered that recruits were joining in high numbers, allowing the recruiters to be selective.

Simple-minded or uneducated individuals are not high on the

list as potential recruits for the international terror organizations. They want men who choose to join the organization, not ones that feel it is their last resort. The poor and desperate may be attempting to join international extremist groups, but they are likely not being selected (69,70).

This chapter explores social issues within the United States and their relationships with terrorism. Preventing terrorism is paramount to winning the war. While there is no agreement on the root cause, there is little doubt that social issues have a strong relationship with terrorism (71,72). President George W. Bush expressed as much in 2002 when he stated that poverty and oppression led to hopelessness and terrorism (73).

As a society, we want to believe the radicalized individual is socially awkward, uneducated, lacking healthy relationships, and for all intents and purposes, psychologically damaged. We find it difficult to fathom that an educated, sane individual would take up arms against their fellow Americans (64).

Terrorism researchers have found a relationship between social inequities and terrorism, but there is rarely a consensus among them. Inequalities relating to socioeconomic levels, education, economic opportunity, and favorable living conditions have greater impact on the poor, minorities, women, and the elderly. Promoting economic equality, supporting the victims of social inequalities, and building healthy communities may begin to curb the growth of terrorism in the United States (72).

Social issues in the US include, but are not limited to, poverty, drug abuse, unemployment, racism and discrimination. People are often born into a particular social condition and are unable to reach beyond their familial status. Typically, social problems disproportionately affect people who share characteristics such as race, religion, economic status or geographic location, and are the result of factors beyond an individual's control.

Several researchers have suggested that poverty and income inequality are factors that increase terrorism, and the media, as well as the public, are quick to blame social issues for terrorism. Several of the September 11 hijackers were on the European welfare system (71). Reaction to inequity is not restricted to the poor. The middle class also complains of being deprived and suffering injustice, and the perception of inequity can be just as harmful as actual injustice (74,75). Victims of inequity and injustice, or perceived injustice may turn their grievances into acts of terror and align themselves with domestic terrorists (71,76,77).

One of the driving forces that steers recruits toward terror organizations appears to be frustration, incensed by the gap between what one expects to achieve and what is achieved (78). One driving expectation is success in employment, to include job satisfaction and significant salaries, specifically if they are well prepared, such as having advanced education. Moreover, this gap between expectation and achievement will turn a person toward terrorism quicker than the actual social state of the individual. The disconnect causes frustration and discontent, leading to aggression.

Some specific social issues that have been linked to terrorism are highlighted in the following sections. We do not intend to provide solutions or even present an exhaustive review of each issue, but wish to introduce the reader to current thoughts and opinions, along with suggestions for reducing the contribution of each issue to terrorism.

Economy (Social Classes)

Terrorists originate in countries that are politically repressed, and they target prosperous countries (69). The evidence that connects terrorism and income levels, however, is deficient (79). Economic deprivation is suggested as one factor that causes people to seek terror groups. Extremists are expected to seek out frustrated youths and steer them toward a common enemy, which may be wealthy people, groups, or countries.

Economic and social turmoil can result in the radicalization of society (80). Some scholars even believe that economic growth that results from technological advancement can incite people to support terrorism. There is a natural resistance to change, especially when people feel they cannot keep up with the changes. It is common to feel lost, confused, or to grow frustrated as they endeavor to keep up. One becomes nostalgic for a simpler life and believes that a radical change in lifestyle will help. Technological advancements can restructure the labor market and those who cannot keep up with the changes find themselves unemployed. Exasperation thus increases along with poverty.

As far back as 1977, it was recognized that a large number of radicalized terrorists are from the middle or upper class (65). This seems to suggest that the effort to achieve one's expectations may not be important for radicalization. On the contrary, someone born into the working class is more likely to accept the working-class strife as a normal part of life. Their expectations of achievement may be lower because all of the people around them are striving to improve their circumstances, but rarely succeed. People born into the upper echelons of the middle or upper class are surrounded by successful peers who continue to increase their wealth. When the effort to measure-up seems unfairly difficult, a person can quickly become frustrated and blame the authorities, like community or government leaders, for creating barriers to their success.

In this research, we examined the professions (see the previous chapter) and resultant social classes of the terrorists. Initially, it seemed that more of the American terrorists were from the working class. Overall, fifty-four percent were working class; forty-six percent of males and thirty-one of females (see Figures 4 and 5). Sixteen percent of the terrorists, however, were college students, and we can assume that college graduates will become professionals and thus fit into the middle or upper class.

The expected composition becomes more balanced if you add together the students, middle, and upper class: forty-six percent compared to fifty-four percent in the working class. The impulse that drives radicalization or increases susceptibility to recruitment by terror organizations, therefore, appears not to be centered on a particular economic class, but with some consternation that is common between classes.

The frustration might come from the working class struggling to reach a more comfortable lifestyle that seems out of reach. It might be the working and middle class feeling that they can never reach a higher class. It might be from those in any class who suffer loss during difficult economic situations. Members of any economic class can suffer from real or perceived inequity in the fight for a comfortable life.

Poverty

If poverty breeds terrorism, we would see a preponderance of terrorists in poverty-stricken areas, but in fact, we see a preference for more prosperous countries (63). Terrorism researchers have debated poverty and its influence on terrorism, just as they have with education. Not everyone agrees with the assumption that poverty breeds terrorism and evidence has been presented against such a relationship (63).

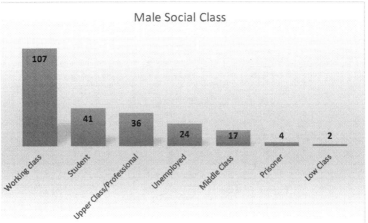

Figure 4: The number of male American terrorists identified in each social class or position indicated.

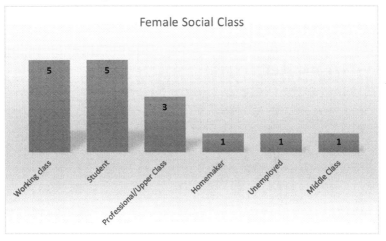

Figure 5: The number of female American terrorists in each social classes or position indicated.

Poverty on its own may not lead a person to terrorism, but it does influence politics, breed corruption, and can be used to repress a country's people. Those factors will produce the same frustration and perceived feeling of helplessness described above, which could increase terrorism.

Political Freedom

According to Krueger & Maleckova (63), terrorism is derived from the perceived lack of political freedom. The goal of a political terrorist is to enact a change or fix a problem with the government that will improve conditions for the broader population, but he or she wants an audience and seeks approval and acceptance from others (6).

Democracies offer their citizens a method to achieve their goals through nonviolent means, but the path is often difficult. The many hurdles standing between them and success can be perceived as a method to suppress the public. Autocracies can repress their citizens without fear of overstepping the law, but such actions will also create a society of struggling, frustrated, and enraged individuals. There is a positive relationship between the rate of terrorist incidents and the lack of political freedom (79).

Political freedom is essential to any democracy, and the U.S. has a long and proud history of political freedom: every citizen has the right and the means to influence the way the country is governed. There is, however, a sense that such freedom has been eroded. The dominance of two major political parties seems insurmountable due to their supremacy at the state and federal level, their great financial resources, and the rules they enact which limit any possible influence from smaller parties. These two parties have controlled the U.S. government for over a century and a half. Could that dominance be viewed as political oppression?

The division between the parties and its accompanying animosity appears to be increasing as they take polar positions on controversial issues. For example, The Republican Party opposes abortion and federal regulation of businesses, supports a flat tax, and believes that wages should be set by the market. The Democratic Party supports a woman's right to abortion and federal regulation to protect consumers, insists on a progressive tax, and supports a minimum wage. Each party strives to block efforts by the other to accomplish its goals, sometimes inhibiting the functioning of the government in the form of government shutdowns or blocking the normal and legal nomination process for government appointments.

Over the last twenty-two years, the U.S. has had two Republican and two Democratic Presidents. During Democratic President William Clinton's two terms, anti-government patriot groups declined from over 800 to less than 200, and it remained that low throughout Republican President George W. Bush's two terms (81). In 2009, the country elected its first President of (confirmed) recent African descent, Democratic President Barack Obama. The number of anti-government patriot groups spiked, reaching over 1300 by the end of his first term (Ibid). That number was under 700 by the time Republican President Donald Trump took office in 2017 (Ibid).

Many factors are involved in the anti-government movements. In the case of patriot groups or militias, their formation was fueled by the perception of increased government regulation and/or a threat to their right to bear firearms (Ibid). Dissatisfaction or distrust in the U.S. government appears to have peaked; however, when an African-American family lived in the White house, suggesting some racial motivation was involved.

88

In 2008, Paul Schlesselman and Daniel Cowart planned to murder eighty-eight African Americans (symbolic for Heil Hitler, "H" being the eighth letter of the alphabet) at an unidentified school and behead fourteen of them (symbolic of the fourteen-word White Supremacist mantra), and end their rampage by assassinating a Presidential candidate, at that time, Barack Obama. Christopher Lee Cornell was arrested in 2015 when an FBI informant revealed his plot to attack the U.S. Capitol and assassinate President Obama during his state of the Union address. American citizens charged with acts related to terrorism during President Obama's tenure that appear less racist and more politically motivated include Yonathan Melaku who shot at the Pentagon and other military facilities in 2010, and Rezwan Ferdaus who planned to fly explosive-laden drones into the Pentagon and the Capitol in 2011.

President Donald Trump has been accused of fanning the flames of racism and the Alt-right movement. His nationalist campaign rhetoric and Presidential policies as well as his apparent pandering to alt-right leaders has encouraged groups who promote white nationalism, to the detriment of non-white Americans (82). During the writing of this book, President Trump has been in office for less than two years, and so it is difficult to measure the trends in terrorism related to his presidency. It appears, however, that the number of antigovernment and Alt-right groups is not rising, but membership in those groups is increasing (Ibid). This may be due to the perception of having a sympathetic ear in the white house, or perhaps those numbers are rising in support for the President.

In October 2018, Cesar Sayoc mailed bombs to outspoken critics of President Trump. He was charged with sending at least fourteen homemade bombs along with photos of their recipients with a red "X" through them. The targets included former President Barack Obama and former Secretary of State

Hillary Clinton. The militia group, Georgia Security Force III%, has proclaimed their willingness to back President Trump with the use of force if necessary.

Race, Gender, and Sexuality

Committing an act of terror on an individual, due to their race or gender is not novel in the United States. Hate groups have had a strong foothold since the creation of the Ku Klux Klan (KKK) in 1866 (83). The Southern Poverty Law Center estimates that there are 892 White Supremacist groups or white nationalist groups in the United States (84). Anti-Muslim hate groups are new to the United States, most of them formed in the aftermath of Sept. 11, 2001. As a country, the U.S. has increased its acceptance of sexual differences, but this new acceptance has also spawned new hate groups.

Racial profiling is the exercise of targeting individuals based on their race or ethnicity in the belief that specific demographics indicate who is likely to engage in unlawful behavior, such as terrorism (85). Some feel that racial profiling is offensive and in direct opposition to the Fourth Amendment, in particular, the act of searching an individual based on their ethnicity, without cause or proof. Nevertheless, ascertaining the race or ethnicity from a witness will help in capturing a potential terror suspect and is in concurrence with the Fourth Amendment (86).

At what point does the potential risk make it allowable to racially profile, including the search of peoples' property based on their ethnicity? Most would think it reasonable when boarding an airplane, that a male from the Middle East between the ages of eighteen and forty, and his baggage, be searched more extensively than others. That, however, is terrorist profiling and it does in fact go against the Fourth

Amendment, which states that the person must pose a real threat before they are treated like one (Ibid).

As of December 2018, 483 male and 36 female Americans were charged with acts related to terrorism since 9/11. Males outnumber the females and as pointed out already, almost half of the female, American terrorists were married to terrorists; half of those were involved in terrorism with their husbands.

American Terrorists and Gender

Gender	Sample Size
Male	483
Female	36

Table 5: Gender and Terrorism

Thanks to profiling, female terrorists can avoid suspicion easier than their male counterparts, but their ability to act covertly is not all that sets women apart as terrorists. They also have a different ideology, often joining terrorist groups to enact changes and participate at the domestic level rather than internationally (87).

It is common to associate terrorism with people of Middle Eastern descent, but there are more Caucasian Americans in the 198 terrorists who have been in the U.S. for two or more generations (see Figure 6). In fact, there are more multi-generational, Caucasian-American terrorists than the other ethnicities combined. Fifty-eight percent of the overall terrorists (see Figure 6) and of the females (see Figure 7) were Caucasian. There were only eighteen multi-generational females: thirteen were Caucasian (seventy-two percent), four were African-American, and one was Latino.

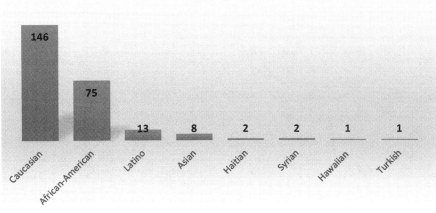

Figure 6: *The number of American-born, multi-generational terrorists in each of the indicated ethnic groups.*

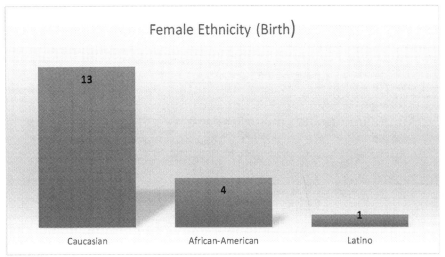

Figure 7: *The number of female, multi-generational, American-born terrorists in each of the indicated ethnic groups.*

Religion

Another misconception is that all terrorists are Islamic militants. Not all of the people who join Jihadist groups are religious or do so for religious reasons. Mohammed Emwazi, also known as Jihadi John, was a British citizen who became a member of the Islamic State and joined their forces fighting in Syria. He was not inspired by religion, but by perceived persecution by the British government (88). Religious terrorists may be motivated by religion, but they are also driven by politics, which clouds any attempt at distinguishing the two motivations (80).

On occasion, religion is the only thread that binds a group together, feeding their fuel to harm. The 1993 World Trade Center bombings are an example of four men who were brought together to accomplish a task with religion being their only common thread (6).

Despite having different religions, many of the terrorists in and outside of the United States believe that their acts of terror are sanctioned by a higher being (80). In 1995, less than fifty percent of foreign terrorist organizations were motivated by a religious agenda (6), but the death and destruction caused by those groups was greater than any other. It is conceivable to believe their greater lethality is connected to their value system (Ibid). Religious groups are not concerned with the perceptions of people outside their faith. They transcend such humanistic thoughts and concern themselves only with the godliness of the act, and the blessing they will receive by committing it. They believe that as religious martyrs, they are cleaning up the world, removing or recruiting non-believers, and they typically seek the blessing or endorsement of their holy men.

The motivation to join a religious terrorist group may come

from the fear of potential disaster or an impending crisis (80). Social inequity may also steer the disenfranchised toward religious groups (76). Some religious communities with no ties to terrorism offer social services to lessen the feelings of inequity, but there are fundamentalist churches that offer the same services to lure in new members. Those benefiting from the services feel gratitude toward the church that helped them. Naturally, they join the church and are indoctrinated, and slowly begin altering their ideologies.

In order to determine the religious devotion of American terrorists, we collected information about their rearing, their devotion at the time of their crimes, and their allegiance to terror organizations. If we could not find information about their devotion at the time of arrest, we used their allegiance. We assumed that alignment with an Islamic terror group indicated Islamic devotion. About half (fifty-two percent) of the American terrorists were raised Muslim and another twenty-nine percent converted to Islam prior to committing acts related to terrorism (see figure 8). Nineteen percent were not Muslim. In total, one hundred and forty-two males and ten females converted to Islam, but the conversion to Islam itself may not be what makes a person a terrorist.

Oroszi posits that a "born-again" factor is involved. When someone finds a new way of life, they often reach extremes in their dedication to it. This is true for select diets such as vegan, keto, or raw; exercise programs like yoga, Zumba, CrossFit, or Insanity; and it is most certainly true for religions including Islam, Christianity, Buddhism, and Scientology. This almost zealot-type behavior has the potential to do more harm than good for the individual, and we believe that when any religion is involved, a person experiencing the "born-again" factor becomes susceptible to recruitment into extremist groups.

One way of showing devotion after converting to Islam is to travel to the Middle East and train for jihad. Of those who converted to Islam, fourteen percent attended terrorist training camps. Another eight percent attempted to travel to the Middle East. Overall, seventeen percent of the American terrorists trained at terrorist camps and another four percent tried to travel to the Middle East. Figure 9 shows the location of the training camps that were attended, and Figure 10 shows how many American terrorists trained at camps in various localities.

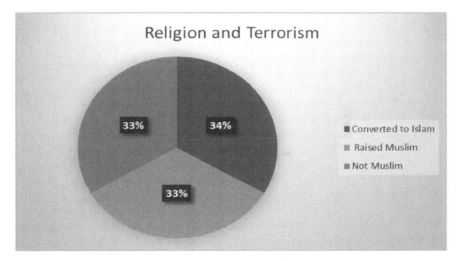

Figure 8: The Distribution of Muslims and non-Muslims in the American Terrorists.

Terrorism Training Camps

Figure 9: World map showing the location of terrorist training camps used by American terrorists. The number of terrorists who trained in each camp increases with the color range.

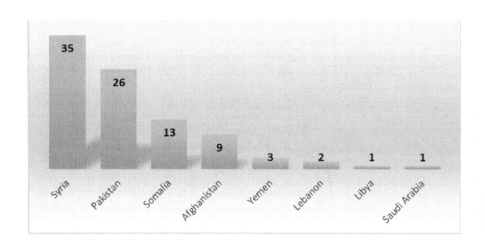

Figure 10: The number of American terrorists who trained at terrorist camps located in the countries indicated.

Awlaki Influence

Anwar al-Awlaki is still recruiting for al-Qaeda, despite being killed by a U.S. drone in 2011, the first drone strike to deliberately target a U.S. citizen. His influence was evident among eighteen percent of the American terrorists who possessed CD's, email correspondences, or their internet history showed views of Awlaki YouTube videos.

Prior to the supporting al-Qaeda Anwar al-Awlaki was a respected Yemeni-American preacher and imam. He was born in Las Cruces, New Mexico in 1971. His father, Nasser al-Awlaki (a former government minister and university president) was attending college in the U.S. when Anwar was born. At the age of seven his family returned to Yemen and he did not return to the U.S. until 1990 when he attended Colorado State University. Anwar received a B.S. in Civil Engineering, a graduate degree in Education but fell short of receiving his Ph.D. in a Human Resources program.

Al-Awlaki served as an Imam at the Arribat al-Islami mosque in San Diego, California, starting in 1996, and at the Dar Al Hijrah in Falls Church, Virginia, in 2001. According to the 9/11 Commission, al-Awlaki befriended three of the 9/11 hijackers. Two of them, Khalid al-Mindhar and Nawaf al-Hazimi, he met at the mosque in California, and the third, Hani Hanjour, at the mosque in Virginia.

His illegal activity apparently began in California, where he was arrested, twice, for soliciting prostitutes. He also served as vice president of the Charitable Society for Social Welfare, which is suspected of funneling money to terrorist organizations.

Al-Awlaki became a senior leader in al-Qaida in the Arabian Peninsula. He instructed Umar Farouk Abdulmutallab, the underwear bomber, in his failed attempt to blow up a civilian airliner over the U.S. and communicated with Major Nidal Hasan before Hassan killed thirteen soldiers at Fort Hood. Tens of thousands of videos featuring Al-Awlaki have been posted on the internet. In 2017 YouTube removed thousands of his videos as part of the site's anti-extremism campaign. His ivieos can still be found on other media sites.

Social Services as a Solution

Social welfare policies can be used to discourage terrorism by reducing inequality and perceived inequity. Spending more on social welfare has the potential to decrease poverty and other issues that spawn extremism. By decreasing inequality and providing support for those suffering economic hardships, the motivation to commit violence, support terrorism, or join religious extremist groups is decreased (71).

The recent mass migrations of refugees have been blamed for an increase in terrorism. The prime minister of Hungary, Viktor Orbán, referred to refugees as the Trojan horse of terrorism. There is conflicting evidence behind such an argument, but two factors seem to be left out of the debate. First, the surge in the population connected to a large migration of refugees will put a strain on most economies and challenge the politics of the community and the country (89). Hardships lead to discontent with lifestyle and with government policies and invite the seeds of violence. The second factor is the harsh treatment of refugees which injects a feeling of inequity and helplessness, which, as already discussed, gives rise to violence and opens the door for extremist ideology and terrorist recruitment.

Some have advocated providing foreign aid to countries known to support terrorist with requirements that the money be used to improve education (90). The idea is to help the disenchanted turn their grievances into a progressive, non-violent political agenda. In that way, their recruitment into a terrorist organization is less likely. While the policy was aimed at the global level, it can also be applied to the community level: social welfare can reduce the likelihood that community members will be targets for terrorist or extremist recruiters.

Conversely, social policies could increase the potential for terrorism. Providing welfare or education could increase awareness of inequalities and cause political discourse (64). Public housing might concentrate the disenchanted and impoverished in a community and facilitate terrorist or antigovernment thoughts and actions (71). In addition, providing education is only half of the equation. If no suitable jobs are available to match the education, which will simply increase the frustration and feelings of being held back.

Chapter Six Summary

In this chapter, we learned that there is no simple description of the mindset of a terrorist. There are economic, political, and religious factors to consider. The American terrorist is not likely to be poor or uneducated, as many expect. In fact, the poor do not have the resources to support terrorism, and some researchers suggest they are too busy putting food on their tables to get caught up in the agenda of others.

When it comes to international terrorist organizations, it seems that they prefer educated recruits. They want people who can think quickly and respond to problems so that the mission will succeed; people who can integrate themselves in an educated society and strike where it will be felt the most. It is plausible to suggest that the recruiters are more interested in people who can lend financial support to the cause. Domestic terrorist organizations have a different tactic, helping those in need in order to earn their loyalty and indoctrinate them into their ideology. The "born-again" factor is likely to have an important role for domestic groups as people strive for perfection in their new-found lifestyle and need kindred spirits to help them on their journey.

More important is the drive for becoming an extremist. It seems credible that the perception of losing political freedom, feelings of economic inequity, and the desire for an exemplary religious dedication can all create a willingness to entertain new options. All one needs is a charismatic leader who presents a convincing argument and lures them into an extremist ideology.

Chapter Seven

Is Your Neighbor a Terrorist?

American terrorists resided in 237 different U.S. localities (cities, towns, or counties) across thirty-six states. If you live in New York City, seventy-two American terrorists shared your residing state and forty-two were your neighbors within the city. The state with the most terrorists was New York (see Table 6 and Figure 11), and the top city for resident terrorists was New York City (see Table 7). Two states had more than one city in the top ten: New York City (number one) and Lackawanna (number ten) in New York; and Columbus (number four) and Cleveland (number six) in Ohio.

The eleven states with the highest number of terrorists each borders a large body of water: an ocean or one of the Great Lakes (see Figure 12). New York, which tops the list, borders three: the Atlantic Ocean, Lake Erie, and Lake Ontario. In fact, in the top nineteen states only one, Arizona with fifteen residents, is land-locked. The only states that border large water bodies but did not have any resident terrorists were New Hampshire, Maine, and Delaware.

Top Ten States Where Terrorists Resided Prior to Arrest

Top Ten States	Number of Terrorists
New York	69
Virginia	44
California	39
Minnesota	36
Ohio	35
Florida	34
Texas	29
Michigan	23
Illinois	21
New Jersey	18

Table 6: Top ten states in which the most American terrorist resided prior to arrest.

Quick Facts about the Top Ten States:

New York borders the Atlantic Ocean, Lake Erie, and Lake Huron. The average age of the New York terrorists was thirty-three. The list included six females, thirteen converts to Islam, and twice as many U.S. citizens by birth than those who were naturalized. Almost half of them were college-educated, but almost half were also in the working class while almost twenty percent were unemployed. The city with the most terrorists was

New York City. Al-Qaeda and ISIS proved to be the favorite international terror organizations for New York terrorists. Terror cells discovered in NY include the ISIS NY Cell, Lackawanna Six or Buffalo Six Cell, and the Newburgh Four.

Top Ten Cities in Which Terrorists Resided Prior to Arrest

Top Cities	# Terrorists
New York City	42
Minneapolis, MN	32
Chicago, IL	15
Columbus, OH	12
Miami, FL	12
Cleveland, OH	10
Falls Church, VA	10
Detroit, MI	9
Houston, TX	9
Lackawanna, NY	9

Table 7: Top cities with the most terrorists residing there prior to arrest.

Virginia borders the Atlantic Ocean and was home to three female terrorists. There were twelve converts to Islam. The average age was twenty-nine. About sixty percent of them were U.S. citizens by birth. Only nineteen percent were college educated, and seventy-three percent were middle to upper class. Falls Church and Alexandra were favorite cities, and ISIS was the favorite international terror organization. Two cells called VA home: the 2003 Virginia Jihad Cell, and D.C. Five or Pakistani Five Cell.

California borders the Pacific Ocean. The average age of a Californian terrorist was 30 and none of them was female.

About sixty percent of them were U.S. citizens by birth. Just over twenty-five percent were college educated and about forty-two percent belonged in the working class and forty-two percent inthe middle and upper class. San Diego was the most popular home city and ISIS, the most popular international terror organization.

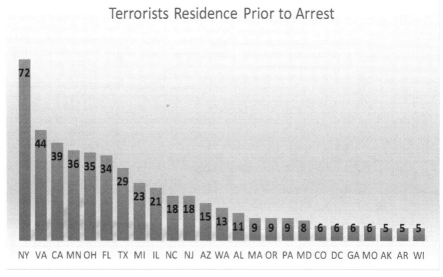

Terrorists Residence Prior to Arrest

Figure 11: The number of terrorists residing in the indicated states at the time of arrest. States with three or fewer resident terrorists that are not included in the graph are CT, HI, IN, KS, LA, MS, NM, OK, RI, and SC.

Minnesota borders Lake Superior. The terrorists from Minnesota averaged twenty-four years old and three of them were female. Only two of them converted to Islam. About twenty-five percent were college educated, but not enough information was available to estimate their social class distribution. Half of the American terrorists from Minnesota were born in the U.S. and half were naturalized citizens. More than sixty-four percent have Somali heritage and eighty percent of them lived in Minneapolis, which is home to a large Somali population. Some estimate it to be the largest Somali population outside of the African horn (91). More than half of the terrorists that resided in MN were aligned with al-Shabaab, a militant terror group that seeks to overthrow the government of Somalia. Most of the convictions were for providing material support or attempting to join a terrorist group overseas.

Ohio borders Lake Erie. Four female terrorists resided there. The average age of the Ohio terrorists was twenty-eight and sixty-four percent of them were born in the U.S. There were six converted to Islam. Only fourteen were college educated and not enough information was available to predict their social class distribution. Columbus was the most popular city and ISIS and Al Fuqra saw the most support from Ohio. Terror cells in Ohio include the Toledo Terror Cell, Columbus Terror Cell, and the Revolutionary People's Group.

Florida borders the Atlantic Ocean. All of the terrorists from Florida were male and their average age was thirty-four. About seventy-seven percent of them were born in the U.S., seventeen converted to Islam, twenty percent were college educated, and the majority belonged to the working class. Miami was the favorite city and ISIS and Al-Qaeda were the most supported international groups. The Miami Liberty Seven Cell and the Jewish Defense League were two cells located in Florida.

Texas borders the Atlantic Ocean via the Gulf of Mexico. Only one female terrorist lived there. The average age of a Texan terrorist was thirty-seven. There were seven converts to Islam, sixty-eight percent were born in the U.S., fifty-five percent were college educated, and about forty-seven percent belonged to each of the working class and middle/upper class. Isis was the most popular terror organization supported, and Houston was home to the most terrorists.

Michigan has borders on three of the Great Lakes: Lake Michigan, Lake Huron, and Lake Erie. Two female terrorists live there. The average age of Michigander terrorists was thirty-two, and fifty-two percent of them were born in the U.S. About thirty percent were college educated and they were split evenly between the working and middle/upper class. There were six converted to Islam. Detroit was the most popular city and ISIS and Al-Qaeda had the most support.

Illinois border Lake Michigan. The average age of the Illinoian terrorists was thirty-two and there were two females. Seventy-six percent were born in the U.S., twenty-nine percent were college educated, and most were in the working class. Chicago was home to the most terrorists and ISIS and Al-Qaeda had the most support.

New Jersey borders the Atlantic Ocean. It had all male terrorists with an average age of thirty-two, and fifty-five percent were born in the U.S. There were twenty-two percent college educated but not enough information was available to determine the social class distribution. ISIS and Al-Qaeda were the most popular international groups. North Bergen was the only city to have more than one terrorist living in it. In fact, NJ is the only state in the top ten that does not have a city in the top ten.

The Citizenship of American Terrorists

There are two ways to become an American citizen. Being born to a U.S. citizen or being born in the U.S. provides automatic citizenship. Otherwise, a person becomes a U.S. citizen through naturalization. The citizenship information was available for ninety-five percent of the American terrorists, and sixty-four percent were born in the U.S. The other thirty-one percent gained citizenship by naturalization after moving to the U.S. (see Figure 13 and Table 8).

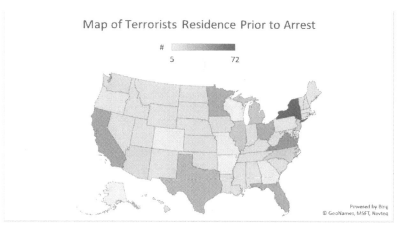

Figure 12: U.S. map showing the number of American terrorists who resided in each state at the time of their arrest. Darker states indicate more terrorists.

Citizenship of Terrorists

Citizenship	# Terrorists
Naturalized	162
U.S. Born	330
Unknown	27
Total	519

Table 8: The Citizenship of American Terrorists

The countries of origin for the parents of the American terrorists are shown in Figure 14. Not only are there twice as many U.S.-born, American terrorists than naturalized, but of the 407 whose parental heritage was found, forty-one percent of them were from the USA. Somalia and Pakistan were next on the list making up less than ten percent of the parental countries each. Also in double digits for the number of terrorists' parents are

Yemen, Egypt, Palestine, Jordan, Afghanistan, and Lebanon.

The U.S. Born Citizens

The most common country from which the parents of the U.S.-born terrorists hail from is the USA (see Figure 16). The next three most common countries, Somalia, Pakistan, and Yemen numbered at less than one tenth the amount from the USA.

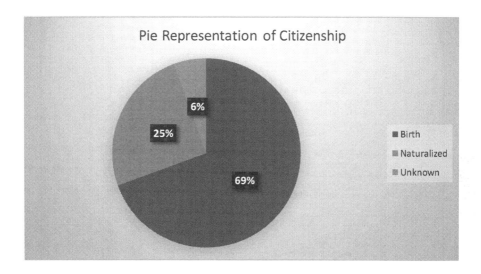

Figure 13: Distribution of citizens by birth versus naturalized citizens for Americans charged with acts related to terrorism.

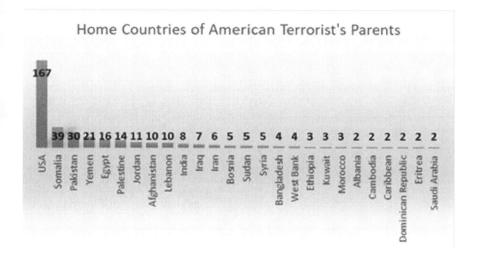

Figure 14: The number of American terrorists with parents from the indicated countries or territories with the exception of the following, each represented by a single American terrorist: Chechnya, China, Cuban, France, Gaza, Ghana, Greece, Guyana, Haiti, Israel, Kenya, Kosovo, Kyrgyzstan, Libya, Macedonia, Mexico, Nicaragua, Panama, Puerto Rico, Greece, Sierra Leone, South Asian, Sri Lanka, and Uzbekistan.

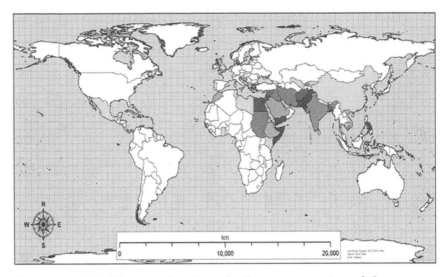

Figure 15: World map showing the home countries of the parents of U.S. born terrorists, excluding the USA. The number of terrorists with parents from each country increases as the shade of red gets darker (Courtesy of Olivia Stone, Ph.D.).

Naturalized Citizens

The country from which the most naturalized, American terrorists derived is Somalia (see Figure 17). Pakistan and Lebanon also reached double digits.

It seems worthwhile to point out how President Trump's Executive Order 13768 (the travel ban) might relate to these statistics. The Order suspended the entry of refugees or immigrants from certain countries based on the potential for terrorists to come from those countries. It specifically banned people from Syria, which is eighth on the list of naturalized and ninth on the list of U.S. born terrorists. The Order also banned countries that did not meet the adjudication standards of the U.S. immigration law. The

Department of Homeland Security listed those countries as Iran (seventh for naturalized, not on the list for U.S. born), Iraq (sixth for naturalized), Libya (not on either list), Somalia (first on naturalized, third on born list), Sudan (tied for eighth on the naturalized list), Syria (tied for eighth naturalized, ninth born), and Yemen (not on either list). Presidential Proclamation 9645 added restrictions on three counties that are not on either list: North Korea, Venezuela, and Chad.

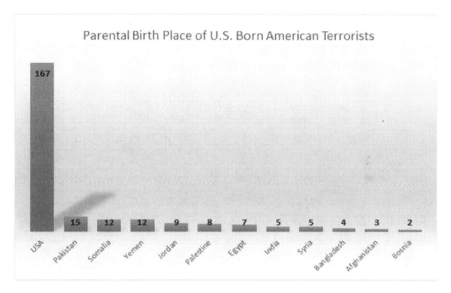

Figure 16: The number of American-born terrorists with parents from each of the countries or territories indicated with the exception of the following, each represented by a single American-born terrorist: Albania, Caribbean, Chechnya, Ethiopia, France, Greece, Guyana, Iran, Iraq, Israel, Kenya, Kosovo, Kuwait, Macedonia, Puerto Rico, and Sierra Leone.

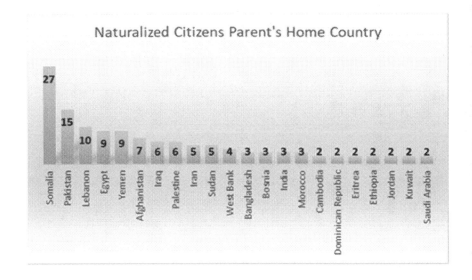

Figure 17: The number of naturalized American terrorists with parents from each of the indicated countries or territories with the exception of the following, each represented by a single naturalized American terrorist: Albania, Caribbean, China, Cuban, Gaza, Ghana, Kyrgyzstan, Libya, Mexico, Nicaragua, Panama, Sri Lanka, and Uzbekistan.

On the surface, this seems to lend some support to the banning of people from at least five of the countries; however, the county's ranking is only one way to visualize the data. For example, a ban on Somalia seems the most justified since the highest number of naturalized terrorists came from Somalia, the country was third on the U.S. born citizens list, sixty-two percent of naturalized terrorists in Minnesota were Somalian, fifty percent in Washington, and thirty-three percent in Ohio. While Somalia ranks high when looking at the individual lists, overall, only three and one-half percent of U.S. born and thirteen percent of naturalized terrorists were Somalian. Remember that thirty-two percent of American terrorists have an American heritage. The statistics do not reveal the number of people that came to the U.S. but did not become terrorists. Nor do they include the number of non-citizen residents from each country that were involved in terrorism. The information presented here should not be used by itself, to support a ban on immigration or travel from certain countries. Instead, it provides a piece of the profile of someone with greater potential to become radicalized, who may need intervention to prevent them from becoming a terrorist.

Chapter Seven Summary

This chapter discussed the distribution of terrorists within the U.S., their citizenship, and their countries of origin. At the state level, we found that the largest number of American terrorists residing in one state is New York, but the city with the most American terrorists is Minneapolis, MN.

The citizenship of the terrorists was surprising: thirty percent of the American terrorists were multi-generational citizens and thirty-four percent of the terrorists are first-generation Americans. For terrorists who were born in the U.S., fifty percent of them had parents who were born in the U.S.

Many imagine that terrorists are people we do not know from far away areas. The information presented in this chapter suggests that terrorists or people who are susceptible to becoming a terrorist might be our neighbors. If we can learn to recognize the signs of someone vulnerable to recruitment into terrorism, perhaps we can also find an intervention that will prevent their radicalization.

Chapter Eight

The American Female Terrorist

Female terrorists were active in the last century. They were joining international groups such as the Provisional Irish Republican Army, the Tamil Tigers of Sri Lanka, and U.S. originated domestic groups like the Ku Klux Klan. It is now commonplace for religious and environmental terrorist groups to recruit women to serve in their ranks, typically in subservient roles. Albeit rarely, females have taken on leadership roles, such as in the American terrorist organization known as the Weathermen (92). It is estimated that thirty percent of those recruited are female (Ibid).

Women are expected to be better terrorists than men because their passion makes them more loyal and often more brutal (93).

Terrorism researcher, Brigitte Nachos (92) disputes that claim, pointing out the lack of evidence that women are more cruel.

Women often join terrorist groups for reasons that differ from men. In 1983, Deborah Galvin (94) speculated that terrorism is part of a natural progression for women due to their traditional roles. One of the most frequent reasons is passion: joining a terrorist organization after falling in love with a member; seeking revenge for the loss, injury, or oppression of a family member or close friend; or seeking justice, having been wronged themselves. The chance for freedom from subservience and domesticity and the cleansing of shame, for example from rape, are also reasons women decide to become terrorists.

The reason women are recruited and utilized by terrorist groups is often due to the general expectation that they are soft, gentle, and innocent (95). Women are expected to be nurturing and to preserve life, not take it, and so they are perceived as less of a threat and not scrutinized as closely or searched as carefully as men.

Women's Role in Terrorism

Support roles for women within the terrorist organizations appear to be the norm (96). There are examples of women moving up the ranks to become leaders, like several South American living in Uruguay, Nicaragua, and El Salvador (Ibid). Often women believe they will have more power, but they find out that the organizations often mirror the very society from which they are trying to escape. During the French and Russian revolutions female terrorists were prevalent, but years later, the German's Red Army Faction, Italy's Red Brigade, and the Cuban Revolution had fewer female participates (Ibid).

The Demographics of a Woman Terrorist

The accurate portrait of a female terrorist depends on many factors. Like their male counterparts, many women turn to terrorism because they feel disenfranchised and discontent with their role in life (97). Industrialization may have a role in driving women to terrorism (98). The growth of industries sent more women into the workforce and increased their opportunities for education, and so women started expecting a better life, but were quickly disappointed to find that they had not escaped the subjugation of gender roles (Ibid). When the socio-political policies of the time failed to bring about new opportunities for women, some of them turned to terrorism (94).

Women have historically held a submissive role in the U.S. and abroad. The subjugation of women is apparent in the workplace where women do not make equal salary and have to work harder for positions of leadership, and at home, where their traditional role is the homemaker. Some women are content with this situation, accepting traditional gender roles with a passion to fulfill their position in life. These women join terror groups because they sympathize with their cause, and are content to provide the group with sewing, cooking, and sexual relief (99).

Current research suggests that religion may influence a woman's decision to join a terrorist organization and define their position in that organization. The rise of liberation theology, for example, convinced Christians of their responsibility to liberate the oppressed and inspired some to join resistance movements (100). The idea of salvation and reuniting with loved ones may also influence a woman's decision to become a terrorist (101).

Some women seek more equality while others want a more dominant role. If they cannot achieve a better standing in their day-to-day life, they become frustrated and may turn to extremism or violence as they seek out organizations that support feminist or socialist philosophies (94). Oppression as a path to terrorism is not new, and not by any means exclusive to females. Historically, many women have turned to violence and terrorism to fight for their right to be a leader. Several political, international terrorist groups involve women in pivotal roles, but terrorist organizations within the United States typically do not put females in prominent roles. There are some examples presented later in this chapter of female leaders that fight for a voice while supporting the cause of their terrorist organization. Interestingly, when Karen Kampwirth interviewed over 200 women activists in Central America (100), only one indicated that a desire for gender equality influenced her decision to become a revolutionary.

Georges-Abeyie (97) predicted that politics would drive a woman to terrorism and that female terrorists would rise from middle-class families, with a few minor exceptions such as the Irish Republican Army (IRA) and some African groups. Reif (96), however, predicted that the middle-class woman is more satisfied with life, and that the lower class is disenchanted with their lives. Personal economics may drive a woman to terrorism, but poverty is not likely the driver. The poor are too busy trying to make ends meet to be bothered by the ambitions of terrorist organizations or to get involved in politics. Moreover, the poorest are typically the least educated with limited access to information, including recruitment propaganda.

The educated woman feels that she deserves more than what life has offered, and she seeks to improve her position. These women feel missed opportunities are rightfully theirs and will seek out ways to improve their lot in life.

The Women of American Terrorism

The women mentioned in this section fall into two categories. They were identified as leaders or outspoken members of terrorist organizations, or they have committed crimes while aligned with either a domestic or international terrorist organization. Many of the females worked alone; however, the majority were married or part of a cell or group.

The Statistics

There have been thirty-six American females charged with acts related to terrorism since 9/11.

Alaa Mohd Abusaad • Amera Akl • Amina Farah Ali • Ariel Bradley • Asia Siddiqui • Colleen Larose (Jihad Jane/Fatima LaRose) • Daniela Greene • Elizabeth Lecron • Hawo Mohamed Hassan • Heather Elizabeth Coffman • Hinda Osman Dhirane • Hoda Muthana (Umm Jihad) • Jaelyn Delshaun Young • Jamie Paulin Ramirez • Judith L. Bruey • Keonna Thomas • Lynn Irene Stewart • Lynn Wingate • Marie Antoinette Castelli • Mediha Medy Salkicevic • Michelle Marie Bastian • Nicole Mansfield • Noelle Velentzas • October Martinique Lewis • Rawdah Abdisalaam (Umm Waqqas) • Roxanne Laura Kopke • Safya Roe Yassin • Samantha Marie Elhassani (Samantha Sally) • Shannon Maureen Conley • Sister of Mohammed Hamzah Khan • Tnuza Jamal Hassan • Traci Elaine Upshur • Zakia Nasrin • Zeinab Taleb-Jedi • Zoobia Shahnaz

Age (At the time of the crime)

The age of female terrorists varied from seventeen to seventy with a mean of thirty-five. About eighty percent of them fall in the age group between seventeen and thirty-four (see Figure 18).

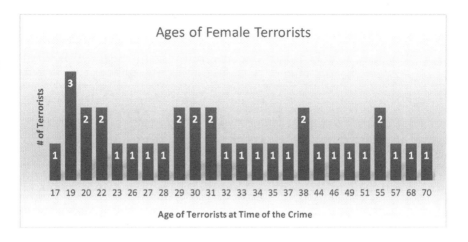

Figure 18: The ages of American females charged with acts related to terrorism at the time of arrest.

Allegiance

The trend in international allegiances for female, American terrorists is similar to the overall allegiances. ISIS was the most popular, followed by al-Qaeda, and then al-Shabaab. Only two females aligned themselves with domestic terrorist organizations, the Jewish Defense League and an unspecified White Supremacist group..

Education

Studies show that education is an essential factor when it comes to recruiting for terrorist organizations. Unfortunately, information, such as education, rarely makes the court documents, police files, or terrorism databases. Eleven of the females arrested for terror-related crimes had some college education or a college degree, three did not have a high school diploma, and the information was not readily available for twenty-one of them. The areas of study for those with college education included liberal arts, nursing, business, chemistry, education, and law. Lynn Irene Stewart had a degree from Rutgers Law and was a defense attorney when she was charged with conspiracy and providing material support to terrorists.

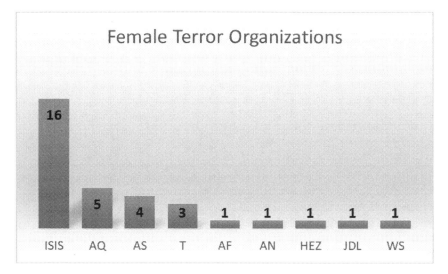

Figure 19: The number of American females charged with acts related to terrorism and their proclaimed allegiances to each of the following terrorist groups: Al-Shabaab (AS), Al Fuqra (AF), Nusra Front or Jabhat al-Nusra (AN), Al-Qaeda (AQ), Hezbollah (Hez), Islamic State of Iraq and Syria (ISIS), Taliban (T), Jewish Defense League (JDL) and unspecified White Supremacists (WS).

Marital Status and Children

In 2014 FBI translator, Daniela Greene married a key ISIS operative she was investigating. Greene told the FBI that she was visiting her parents in Munich, Germany. Instead, she went to Syria and married Denis Cuspert, also known as Deso Dogg, a German rapper, and Abu Talha al-Almani, an ISIS pitchman.

The relationship status was already discussed in Chapter 5

and will only be summarized here. Seventy percent of women involved in terrorism were married and twenty-one percent of them had children. Half of the married female terrorists were married to terrorists. If we include one who divorced a terrorist and two who were engaged to terrorists, fifty-nine percent were involved in a relationship with a terrorist.

Mental Health Issues

No mental health issues were identified in the female terrorists. Such issues are not always recognized, and they can go undiagnosed, but in this sample group of female terrorists there was no indication of mental illness.

Sentence or status

Thirty-six women had been charged with acts related to terrorism by the time this book went to the press. The average length of prison sentence was nearly eight and one-half years and the longest sentence was twenty years. Amina Farah Ali, from Minneapolis, MN, received the twenty-year sentence for multiple counts of providing support to al-Shabaab. When compared to their male counterparts, the women have sentences that are more lenient: their average is thirty-seven percent less than the male average. Only three weapons charges were known, and they involved explosives. Asia Siddiqui and Noelle Velentzas from New York, NY, were building bombs and planning to attack law enforcement officials. Elizabeth Lecron from Toledo, OH, allegedly had bomb-making materials and planned to attack a local bar or restaurant.

Terror Timeline

Terrorism in the U.S. did not start with the acts of 9/11. The

Ku Klux Klan, for example, has been in existence since 1866. Several domestic terror organizations were active during the Vietnam War and the Civil Rights Movement in the 1950's and 1960's. Women were prominent in domestic terrorist movements when Bernardine Dohrn was the leader of the Weather Underground Organization in the late 1960's.

Since 9/11, there have been three surges in terror-related acts: immediately after the 9/11 attack; in 2009/2010 when the economy was in a recession; and 2014/2015 when ISIS was growing and their social media recruiting skills proved to be successful (see Figure 20).

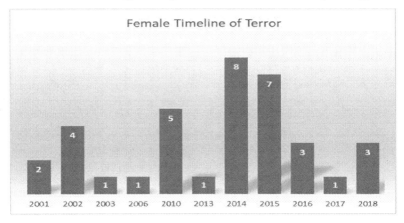

Figure 20: The number of American females charged with acts related to terrorism and the year of arrest from 2001 to 2018.

Historical Female Terrorists

Rachel Pendergraft

Rachel Pendergraft is the daughter of Thomas Robb, an anti-evolution church pastor and prominent leader in the Ku Klux Klan. Pendergraft became an active KKK member and raised her children with similar beliefs. She organized the Soldiers of the Cross-Training Institute in 2013 and co-hosted a cable show as part of her leadership role within the group (102). The institute was focused on recruiting white Christians. Rachel has used social media to spread the KKK message, including Facebook, Twitter, and a Website. Pendergraft has not yet been accused or convicted of crimes related to terrorism, despite her pervasive message of hate. Allegiance: Ku Klux Klan (KKK)

Lisa Turner

Lisa Turner was an outspoken female leader in the Neo-Nazi Group, World Church of the Creator (WTOTC) (103). Turner was the women's information coordinator and produced the World Church of the Creator newsletter, underlining her efforts to increase the female voice within the organization (104). The World Church of the Creator, unlike other domestic, white supremacist, terrorist organizations, recruited women to leadership roles. Turner used social media and the internet to recruit and distribute information, including the Women's Frontier Website. Allegiance: World Church of the Creator (WTOTC)

Kathy Ainsworth

Ainsworth was indoctrinated into a philosophy of racism and segregation by a professor at Mississippi College. She married a man that understood, but did not subscribe to her feelings. She became a member of the Ku Klux Klan while teaching fifth grade at a segregated school and took on Klansman Tommy Tarrants as her lover. They tried to bomb the home of a prominent Jewish citizen in Meridian, MS, but she died from a gunshot during an FBI ambush. Allegiance: Ku Klux Klan

Joanne Chesimard

JoAnne Deborah Byron was born in New York. She grew up living with relatives in North Carolina and sometimes with her mother in New York. She went to college in New York and married activist Louis Chesimard and became involved with the Black Panther Party. She changed her name to Assata Olugbala Shakur and in 1971, joined the Black Liberation Army (BLA).

In 1973 she was arrested and eventually convicted for the murder of a New Jersey state trooper. She was serving a life sentence when members of the BLA helped her escape from prison (105). While she was serving time for murder, she was also wanted for bank robbery, kidnapping, and attempted murder (106).

Chesimard fled to Cuba in 1984, where she was granted political asylum. She was placed on the FBI's Most Wanted Terrorist list in 2013. She is wanted for domestic terrorism, unlawful flight to avoid confinement, and murder. When Fidel Castro died in 2016, there was a renewed effort for extradition to finish serving her jail sentence. Allegiance: Black Liberation Army (BLA)

Diana Oughton

Diana Oughton grew up in an affluent family; her great-grandfather founded the Boy Scouts of America. Her father was a politician and a graduate of Dartmouth. She attended Bryn Mawr as an undergraduate and the University of Michigan (UM) for graduate studies. At UM, Oughton became an active member and leader in the Vietnam war protesting organization, Students for a Democratic Society (SDS). She and her boyfriend,

Bill Ayres, lead a splinter group that they called the Jesse James Gang. When the SDS dissolved, Oughton, Ayres, and their friend Terry Robbins joined the Weather Underground Organization.

Oughton, Robbins, and Theodore "Ted" Gold were assembling a nail bomb in a New York Greenwich Village basement when it exploded prematurely (107). They intended to detonate it in an NCO Club at Fort Dix Army Base. Fellow Weatherman members, Cathy Wilkerson and Kathy Boudin, were in the townhouse at the time of the explosion but were not injured (108). Oughton was indicted posthumously as part of a conspiracy to destroy American society by bombing police, military, and other civic buildings. Oughton was twenty-eight years old at the time of her death. Allegiance: Weathermen aka Weather Underground Organization.

Angela Shannon

Angela Shannon was just nineteen years old in 1993 when she wrote a death threat to Dr. Woodward, an abortion physician.

> *"If I hear you are still killing when I get to town, I will haunt you and your wife day and night and give you no peace. If you continue, I will hunt you down like any other wild beast and kill you."*

Angela's father was married to another woman when her mother, Shelley, gave birth to her. Shelley (see next profile) was inspired by Operation Rescue to become an antiabortion activist but drew inspiration from Last Days Ministries who advocated violence against abortion. Angela was home-schooled by her mother, and allegedly brought along to protest and burn abortion clinics. Angela was sentenced in 1997 to four years in prison for her death threat to Dr. Woodward. Her mother was already serving time for attempted murder. Allegiance: Army of God

Shelley Shannon

Rachelle Ranae "Shelley" Shannon was inspired by Last Days Ministries and Operation Rescue to begin protesting and blocking abortion clinics. In 1992 she began a campaign of arson and acid attacks. Shelley reportedly edited manuals for the Army of God and corresponded with members who were convicted of terrorist acts. In 1993, she shot an abortion doctor, George Tiller, and was sentenced to eleven years for attempted murder. Two years later, her sentence was extended another twenty years after she pled guilty to vandalism, arson, and bombings at several clinics (109). During sentencing, Judge Redden said, "Though I am loathed to call anyone a terrorist, you are a terrorist." Shannon served twenty-five years in federal prison and six months in a half-way house and was freed on November 7, 2018 (110). Allegiance: Army of God

Susan Stern

Susan Tanenbaum was born in Brooklyn and came from a wealthy family (111). She earned an undergraduate degree in liberal arts, married Robert Stern, and then taught 6th grade while attending graduate school. After she was expelled, for teaching communist and subversive doctrines, she moved to Washington with her husband. There they joined the Students for a Democratic Society (SDS). Stern earned a Master of science degree in social services, separated from her husband, and attended protests and conventions as a member of the SDS and then as a member of the Weather Underground Organization.

While protesting the treatment of the Chicago seven in 1970, Stern and seven others were arrested and charged with conspiracy to plan a riot. One of the defendants disappeared before trial and was never seen again, and those who went to trial became known as the Seattle Seven. The trial was disrupted, eventually declared a mistrial, and the seven were cited for being in contempt of court. In exchange for not challenging the contempt charges, the other charges were dropped, and the defendants served minimal sentences.

Stern wrote a memoir entitled "With the Weathermen: The Personal Journey of a Revolutionary Woman," in which she described her experience. She died in 1976 of heart seizures that may have been related to drug use. Allegiance: Weathermen aka Weather Underground Organization (WUO)

Chapter Eight Summary

This chapter shared information from the current literature, and media sources to paint the picture of an American female terrorist. One of the most differentiating things that separate the males from the females is alliances. All the females pledged their allegiance to a terrorist organization, whereas near ten percent of the males committed acts without aligning with a known terror organization.

The thirty-six women charged with acts related to terrorism since 9/11 were, on average, thirty-five years old and vary greatly in their level of education. No mental health issues were identified. Most of them were married, half of them married to terrorists. The average prison sentence was approximately eight- and one-half years, thirty-seven percent less than their male counterparts.

Female terrorists have been active since the 1960s. Religious, environmentalist and White Supremacist organizations are actively recruiting female members. Women typically join terrorist groups for reasons of passion: they fall in love with a member of a terrorist organization, they seek revenge; or they seek redemption. Some try to escape domesticity, while others seek to fill that role for the organization. Women have achieved leadership roles in some organizations, but more often are used in domestic or covert roles.

Chapter Nine

The American Male Terrorist

Humans, as a species, feel there is something that makes every one of us unique. Our young male citizens are no different. As fledgling adults, they often feel the need for adventure and camaraderie. They often experience a desire to do something grand along with a craving to be heroes. Transiting from their parents' house to a state of independence can be a freedom for the young men. This autonomy can lead to excessive drinking, playing video games, as well as working and progressing through adulthood. In many circumstances, it is a time to reflect on their philosophies of religion, life, and culture. They can separate from the ideologies of their parents and form their own. It is an opportune time for recruitment by extremist organizations.

This chapter examines the demographics of male, U.S. citizens who were charged with crimes related to terrorism. Although terrorism is not new, the 9/11 attack marked a change in history and began the war on terror. This study, therefore, only examines the 483 males who were charged since 9/11.

Terror Timeline

The number of male, U.S. Citizens charged as terrorists during each year since 9/11 is shown in Figure 21. The figure reveals three spikes in activity. Immediately after 9/11, in 2002 and into 2003, al-Qaeda inspired U.S. citizens took up arms in abundance. The next spike is in 2009. The U.S. economy was in a recession during 2007 – 2009, and an increase in terrorism is expected to accompany difficult times such as during a recession (112); however, President Barak Obama was sworn in as the 44th President in January 2009. His position as the most powerful man in the world upset many and may have inspired citizens to take up arms against their fellow citizens. The third spike occurs in 2015, which may be connected to the rapid growth of ISIS during that time. The male timeline is similar to the female timeline presented in the previous chapter (see Figure 20, Chapter 8).

The Age of Male Terrorists

The American males that committed acts related to terror are quite diverse in their ages, fifteen to eighty-nine years old with a mean of thirty-two (see Figure 22). About eighty percent of them were between fifteen and forty-three years old.

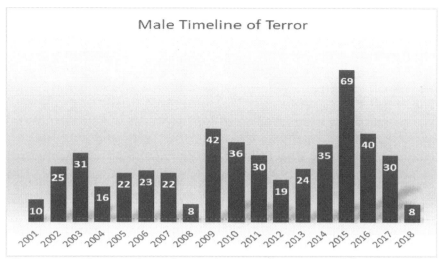

Figure 21: The number of American males arrested for acts related to terrorism and the years of arrest from 2001 to 2018.

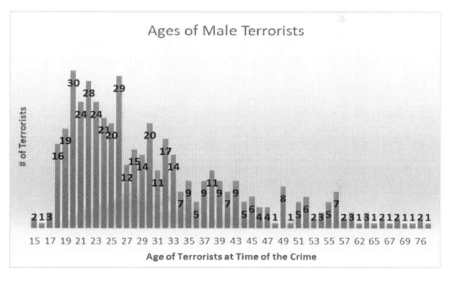

Figure 22: The ages of American males arrested for acts related to terrorism at the time of arrest.

Allegiance

Allegiance to a foreign or domestic organization can offer the would-be terrorist a feeling of family or unity, as if belonging to a brotherhood.

Donald Morgan joined the military but could not finish boot camp. He then tried law enforcement, but he was unhappy with the perceived lack of brotherhood, and his position was terminated after a couple of years. His marriage ended in divorce and he became a Muslim about a year later. When he decided to be more serious about his faith, he was radicalized and aligned with ISIS.

Domestic terror organizations seem to be not as successful in recruiting members as the international groups. We found fifty-five allegiances to domestic groups in the American males (see Figure 23), but there were 424 aligned with international groups (see Figure 24). Alternatively, perhaps those aligned with domestic groups are harder to catch or are less likely to be arrested. In the domestic groups, the alt-right were most successful with seven claiming allegiance to unspecified white supremacist groups, two Nazis, and one with the National Socialists Movement.

Political groups had thirty-eight associated with them. One group, Revolutionary People's Group, started as part of the peaceful, Occupy Wall Street movement. They were not satisfied with a peaceful movement and so they set out to bomb a bridge connecting two affluent neighborhoods in Cleveland, Ohio.

The ideological Jewish Defense League and religious Jam'iyyat Ul-Islam Is-Saheeh also found their way onto the list of American male terrorists.

ISIS and al-Qaeda were the top international terrorist organizations, having one hundred and forty-nine and one hundred and eleven men aligned with them, respectively (see Figure 24). The next three on the international list, al-Shabaab, the Taliban, and Lashkar-e-Tayyiba, added together did not match ISIS or al-Qaeda.

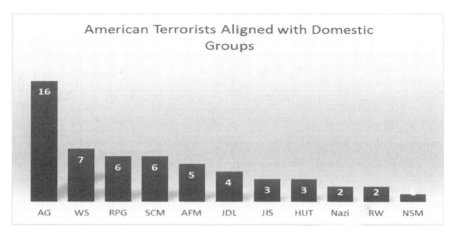

Figure 23: Terrorists Aligned With Domestic Organizations. Anti-Government (AG), White Supremacy (WS), Revolution People's Party (RPP), The Sovereign Citizens Movement (SCM), Jewish Defense League (JDL), Jam'iyyat Ul-Islam Is-Saheeh (JIS), Nazi Party (Nazi), Right Wing (RW), and the National Socialist Movement (NSM).

Education

As pointed out in the previous chapter, information about education is often not available. We found that one hundred and sixty of the males in this study had some college education or earned a degree and one hundred and eleven did not. No information was located for two hundred and twelve males charged with acts of terror. This means that for those with information available, fifty-nine percent had an advanced education.

Married/Children

As already discussed in Chapter 5. Sixteen percent of men were married, and nine percent of the men were fathers.

Male Terrorist Mental Health

The mental fitness of a terrorist is a mystery to many. We want the terrorists to have mental issues because we do not want to believe anyone without mental issues would commit such atrocities. It may yet be true; however, only fifty-eight of the American men in this study (eleven- and one-half percent) were diagnosed with mental health issues. The issues included post-traumatic stress disorder, developmental disability, depression, bipolar disorder, autism, ADHD, and hallucinations.

Mohamed Amiin Ali Roble experienced post-traumatic stress disorder from being on the bus during a bridge collapse at age ten. Rasel Raihan (Abu Abdullah al-Amriki), Jason Michael Ludke and Mohammad Youssuf Abdulazeez, suffered from depression. Harlem Suarez had a possible developmental disability. Mahin Khan and Jason Michael Ludke had autism.

Santos Colon Jr. was institutionalized after arrest as a juvenile and held until age twenty-one. David Headley (Daood Sayed Gilani), Hasan Akbar, Rezwan Ferdaus, James Elshafay, Aman Hassan Yemer, and Naveed Afzal Haq were diagnosed before they committed their crimes. Roger Stockham, Walli Mujahidh, Tahmeed Ahmad, Clifford L. Cousins, Iyman Faris, Muhammed Taheri-Azar, and Emerson Begolly were all hospitalized before committing their crimes or before arrest. Yonathan Melaku was diagnosed after his crime.

Sentence/Status

There was no identifiable, direct correlation between the charges and the sentences. The sentences ranged from days to life, even if no related deaths occurred. Life sentences were handed to twenty of the men. There are seventeen on the list still waiting for their trial or sentencing. Three of the men committed suicide. Seven were killed during arrest and another two were killed by a drone strike. Three more died before sentencing and two were given a death sentence. Five remain as fugitives.

The average sentence length for men was thirteen years. The men typically receive a longer sentence than woman. Research shows that there is a long-standing gender gap related to sentences and sentence length. For this study the women received an approximate twenty-five percent reduced sentence compared to their male counterparts. When this calculation was done in 2015 the gap was much larger, nearly fifty percent. This leads us to believe that the judicial system has begun to regard the females as terrorists themselves, and not as victims.

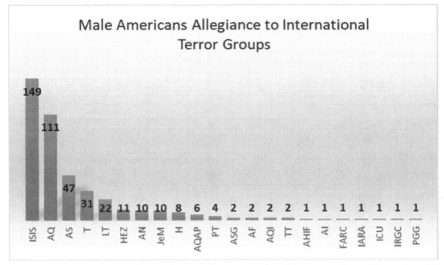

Figure 24 The number of American male citizens who aligned with the following International terror organizations: Al Fuqra (AF); Al Haramain Islamic Foundation (AHIF); Ansar al-Islam (AI); Nusra Front or Jabhat al-Nusra (AN); Al-Qaeda (AQ); Al-Qaeda in the Arabian Peninsula (AQAP); Al-Qaeda in Iraq (AQI); Al-Shabaab (AS); Abu Sayyaf Group (ASG); Hamas (H); Hezbollah (Hez); Iranian Islamic Revolutionary Guard Corps (IRGC); Islamic State of Iraq and Syria (ISIS/ISIL); Jaish-e-Mohammed (JeM); Lashkar-e-Tayyiba (LT); Pakistan Taliban (PT); Taliban (T); and the Tamil Tigers (TT).

Chapter Nine Summary

This chapter presented the demographics of the American male terrorist. They were between fifteen and ninety-three years-of-age with an average of thirty-two. About fifty-nine percent had advanced education. Only sixteen percent were married and nine-percent had children. Approximately eleven percent had identified mental health issues. The average prison sentence was thirteen years.

One possible way to stop a terrorist group from recruiting

American citizens is to recognize a susceptible person and provide them with better alternatives. We believe that by defining the profile of the American terrorist, parents, coaches, teachers, and family members will be empowered to recognize the potential for radicalization in individuals and to intervene, steering them down a better path. We used the demographics of those already charged with crimes related to terrorism to build this profile. The available data included 519 U.S. citizens charged with acts related to terrorism since 9/11. The males outnumbered the females by more than thirteen-fold (483 male, 36 female), making their demographic more impactful.

Chapter Ten

Recognizing a Developing Terrorist

Our enemy ais terrorism and the violence that terrorists perpetrate, often premeditated, against the innocent (113). Law enforcement professionals work hard to stop terrorists, and they are often successful. We can help through accurate profiling. Terrorist profiling is the science of identifying qualities that predict the probability that an individual will become a terrorist. Perhaps, even reveal the primary target for recruitment into terrorist organizations.

There is some debate over the effectiveness of profiling (114). A profile based on race ignores the fact that many who are the same race are not, and will never be terrorists, and that people of other races do become terrorists. If based on gender, it allows females to be furtive and provides an opportunity for the greater success experienced by some historical, female terrorists. A profile based on age is problematic because the mean age, typically young, is different between organizations, but the leaders tend to be older and would not fall within such a profile. Psychological profiling, which has been somewhat successful in other criminal areas, has not produced a single terrorist personality that fits all the known terrorists. Jonathan Rae, a crisis management director, suggests that any successful profile will have to be context-specific and ephemeral (Ibid).

Terrorist profiling must rely on a systematic study to determine reproducible indicators. Those indicators can then become a red flag to warn family, teachers, coaches, friends, and acquaintances that an individual may be susceptible to radicalization or may already be a terrorist. Having recognized the danger, the attentive contact can palliate the motivations that are most likely to cause radicalization and lead to an act of terrorism.

Historical Terrorist Profiling

This is, of course, not the first time a terrorist profile has been described. The markers we used for the profile came from a larger sample group that was limited to U.S. citizens, and we examined more potential markers than previous studies, but the profiles were similar.

In 1980 B.M. Jenkins (115) proposed a terrorist profile in 1980: single male from a middle- or upper-class family in his early twenties with some university education,with a strong likelihood that they are recruited at the university. Dingley (116) put forth his "classic" terrorist profile in 1997: twenty-two to twenty-five years old and from an urban area, raised in a liberal, middle- to upper-class household.

In their article, "Profile of a Terrorist," Russell and Miller (65) presented a profile based on the information available in news media about 350 terrorists in eighteen different Middle Eastern, Latin American, Western European countries, and Japan. Their profile was a single male, aged twenty-two to twenty-four, with some college education, typically in the humanities, and coming from an affluent, middle, or upper-class family. They identified universities as a recruiting center because the individuals were introduced to new ideas, but defined frustration and anarchist or nihilist ideas as the impetus for radicalization.

In Chapter 5, we explained our findings about the education, profession, and marital status of American terrorists. Chapter 6 discussed the potential influence of social class, poverty, political freedom, religion, and race and gender on radicalization. Chapter 7 explored the relationship between terrorism and resident locality, citizenship, and country of origin. In Chapters 8 and 9 we presented the data on female and male, American terrorists, respectively. The demographics on male and female Americans who were charged with crimes related to terrorism included their age, education, marital status, mental health, and the terrorist organizations that they admired or to which they claimed allegiance. The remainder of this chapter will present the profile of an American terrorist based on the data we collected and on the historic profiles presented above.

The Profile

1. Male

We found that ninety percent of the U.S. citizens charged with acts related to terrorism were male (see Figure 25). Profiles in the literature reported the same (65,115,116). Historically, men carry out the bulk of terrorist acts in the U.S., but by focusing on men as potential perpetrators, women will find it easier to be clandestine terrorists (see Chapter 8). The ability of women to avoid suspicion may increase their recruitment in the future, particularly as suicide bombers (117). Nevertheless, male terrorists are more abundant, and their motivation tends to be nationalistic or religious in nature, whereas a women's motivation to become a terrorist of more often personal, such as love or vengeance (118,119). This suggests that women are less likely to become terrorists independent of their husbands, companions, or family.

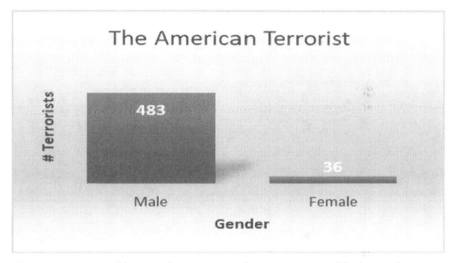

Figure 25: Profile Marker #1, males are more likely to become terrorists (N=519).

2. Age 15-40

This age bracket included eighty percent of the American citizens charged with terror-related acts. Previous research in the literature suggested a much younger age range, twenty-two to twenty-five (65,116). The overall age range and mean for all the American terrorists in this study and for the men alone was the same: fifteen to eighty-nine years-old with a mean of thirty-two (see Figure 26). The most common age was twenty years old. Interestingly, alignment with terrorist organizations appeared to be age-dependent: younger males frequently aligned with international terror group, while older men aligned with domestic groups or acted independently.

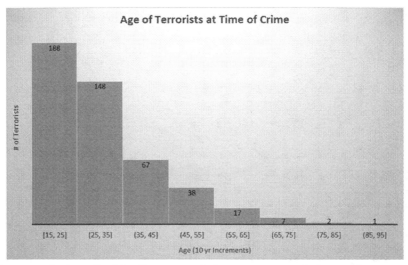

Figure 26: Profile Marker #2, eighty percent of the male, American terrorists were between the ages of fifteen and forty years old. The mean was thirty-two years old, and the most frequent age was twenty years old.

3. Educated (increased risk if unemployed)

Others have also reported that terrorists frequently have a postsecondary education (65,115). In this data set, sixty-one percent of male American terrorists had some college education (see Figure 27). More than half of those were in STEM fields (see Figure 28). Studies in humanities or social sciences have been more common in previous studies (65), but Gambetta and

Hertog reported a disproportionate number of radical Islamists with engineering backgrounds (120). Sageman also found, in 2004, that most terrorists had advanced studies in science and technology (66).

The connection between education and terrorism was discussed in Chapter 5. A less educated person has fewer opportunities for gainful employment and works hard for little salary making it difficult to enjoy life; however, they are likely to accept part of the blame for their lot in life. When an individual with a postsecondary education finds themselves unemployed or working in positions beneath their training or education, transfers the blame to whomever they perceive is holding them back. The college-educated individual expects to achieve a certain measure of success because they put in the work that was expected of them (postsecondary education). They blame the government or community leaders, for example, for creating barriers to their success. The gap between expectation and actual achievement can turn a person to terrorism quicker than the actual social state of the person.

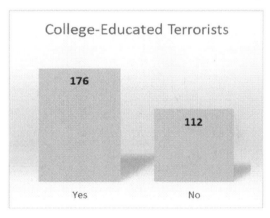

Figure 27: Profile Marker #3, one hundred and seventy-six of the American male terrorists were confirmed to have some college experience while one hundred and twelve were confirmed to not

have any college education.

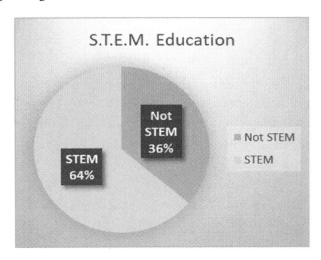

Figure 28: Strengthening Profile Marker #3, sixty-four percent of the 94 terrorists with defined majors were in STEM fields.

4. No girlfriend or wife

This study found that eighty-one percent of male Americans charged with acts related to terrorism were not married, they were single or divorced (see Figure 29). Others have also reported that most terrorists are not in relationships (65,115,116,121). Married men may find a voice of reason in their wives, preventing their joining of terrorist groups, or perhaps a sense of family responsibility helps to prevent radicalization. Other researchers support the belief that a man not encumbered by a wife or girlfriend is more likely to commit terrorist acts (122-124). The profile only reflects traditional relationships because to date, no terrorist has identified as gay, bisexual, lesbian, or transgender.

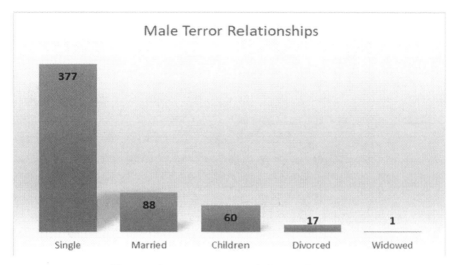

Figure 29: Profile Marker #4, most of the male, American terrorists were single. For this study all males not identified as married, divorced, or widowed were assumed to be single.

5. Raised without a father figure

This background information was not readily available for the American terrorists, but contemporary literature supports the lack of a father figure as an indicator (125-131). The effect of absentee fathers on terrorist potential is similar to that of gang recruitment in American cities (125,132). The family structure is considered the most reliable predictor of male, criminal potential, and that potential increases if the male is fatherless (121). For example, eighteen out of twenty-five of the most commonly cited school shooters since Columbine were reared in broken homes (133). The gang leaders or the leaders of terrorist organizations become a father figure for young men, teaching them to be men and making them soldiers for their cause.

6. From a middle- or upper-class family

Other researchers have asserted that terrorists come from middle- or upper-class families (65,115,116). In this study, we found that the American terrorists were fairly balanced between two groups: the working class, and a group composed of the middle and upper classes and college students (see Chapter 6). The reason terrorists can come from any economic or social class is that everyone, regardless of class, responds negatively to injustice. The middle and upper class can experience injustice, real or perceived, and react in the same way as the working class (74,75,79). As discussed in Chapter 6, the poor are the least likely to become terrorists. They are less likely to be recruited and are too busy trying to put food on their tables to take up the causes of terrorist organizations.

7. Displaced or alienated

There is a tendency for individuals feeling isolated, displaced, alienated and lonely to join terrorist organizations (134-137). Displaced does not necessarily mean they are from another country, but almost one third of the American terrorists in this study were naturalized citizens, having come from other countries (see Chapter 7). Displacement can also refer to moving to another state, or switching between rural, suburban, or urban environments, or a change in lifestyle. Alienation can occur when a neighborhood that is dominated by one ethnicity feels isolated from the surrounding communities. People can feel like they do not fit in and cannot share their opinions or feelings. They become lonely and lose their sense of purpose, their direction. The terrorist organizations promote comradery and offer new purpose, new direction.

8. Angry and/or victimized

Anger and victimization have been cited as motivations for becoming a terrorist (138-141). People who experience inequity in their attempt to succeed are likely to join domestic terrorist groups who share their frustration. People who feel their dignity or humanity has been stolen seek to strike back and redeem themselves.

Some of the radicalized Americans convicted of terrorism were recruited while in prison (142,143). Many prisoners feel that their arrest and/or punishment was unfair or unjustified, and once inside, become victims of the guards or other inmates. Many angry inmates are available for recruiting.

Other Interesting Findings

Some variables did not fit the profile but are interesting to consider when determining the likelihood that a person will join a terrorist organization or engage in terrorist activities.

1. Mental Health:

Our research indicated that eleven- and one-half of the American's arrested for acts related to terrorism were diagnosed with mental illnesses. Large terrorist organizations can be somewhat selective (68), and therefore are likely to screen out many mental illnesses. Every organization wants the most capable people as members, and so anyone perceived as weak or unable to complete tasks are likely to be passed over for membership. Lone wolves, or people acting independent of organized groups, are reported to be over thirteen times more likely to have mental illness than terrorists sponsored by a larger organization (144). Another explanation for the lower than expected number of mental health issues is the lack of detection, diagnosis, and treatment.

2. Military:

Eight- and one-half percent of the terrorists joined the U.S.

military. The Army recruited more than any other military branch, fifty percent of the military terrorists had Army experience, fifty percent joined other branches. The Army is the oldest and largest U.S. military service, and it is supported by two reserve forces: The Army Reserves, and the Army National Guard.

3. Religion:

Religious fanatics involved in terrorism are much more dangerous than the non-religious terrorists (145). Religious terrorists believe they are acting in the name of God and are on the side of good (146). Religious fundamentalism is currently associated with violence, extremism, to include terrorism (147). Of the 519 terrorists two hundred and sixty-nine were raised Muslim and one hundred and fifty-two converted to Islam.

4. Anwar al-Awlaki:

Aliases: Anwar al-Awlaki also spelled al-Aulaqi, al-Awlaqi; Anwar al-'Awlaqī. He was born in New Mexico and raised in California. His parents were from Yemen. Al-Awlaki was killed in a U.S. drone strike in 2011, while he was serving as Osama bin Laden's media adviser and spokesperson. At least eighteen percent of the American citizens charged with acts related to terrorism had Awlaki's CDs, emails, or YouTube videos in their possession.

Chapter Ten Summary

This chapter an 8-marker profile of an individual that is likely to be radicalized. It was based on historical profiles in the literature and statistics from our own study of 519 American terrorists. In addition to the profile four areas of interest, Mental Health, Military, Religion and Anwar al-Awlaki were included in this chapter.

Chapter Eleven

American Terrorists and the Military

The men and women of the United States military are some of the most patriotic people in the country. Many people would be shocked to know that several military men have chosen a path of terrorism during, or after, their time in service to their country. Our data indicates that nearly seven and one-half percent of the American's arrested for acts related to terrorism had military experience, half of whom were in the U.S. Army (see Figure 33). No reason for the transition from the U.S. military to terrorist has been defined, but there are several possible explanations.

Brotherhood

What do the military, law enforcement, and firefighters have in common? They work together for a common goal, protecting and saving people, while risking their lives. Many consider them heroes. Terrorists are similar: they believe in their cause, they want to help those who also believe, and wish to be known as heroes. The youth, who commonly have a feeling of invincibility, make excellent recruits for each of the vocations mentioned above.

Trained Killer

Several of the military terrorists admitted to joining the military so they could learn skills that would make them better killers.

Lost/Alienated

When someone is released from the military after several years of service, they often feel lost. It is the first time some of them have to take care of themselves. Some military can spend their entire paycheck on the day it is received and still have a home, a job, and food on the table. There is limited training to reintegrate back into civilian life after separation.

The thirty-eight veterans varied in age from twenty to eighty-eight years old. Twenty-two military terrorists aligned with international groups and four with domestic groups. The remainder did not identify with a terrorist organization.

Four military members were part of a Virginia Jihad Terror Cell, and one was a member of the Portland Seven Terror Cell. All but three members were born to parents from the United States. Seven of the military men were married, and one was divorced. Post-Traumatic Stress Disorder (PTSD) affects many military personals that return from war. None of those on our list were confirmed to suffer PTSD, but Davis, Harroun, and Teausant were diagnosed with mental illnesses.

Below is a list of thirty-eight military men that took up arms against their countrymen. Twenty-two of them were Army, nine Marines, six Navy and one Air Force.

Terrorists Who Served in the Army

Naser Jason Abdo

Abdo was a Private in the U.S. Army stationed at Ft. Campbell, Kentucky, where he planned to kill high-ranking Army officials while chanting the names of Muslims that had been harmed by the military. When his plan did not work out, he went absent without leave to Ft. Hood, Texas, where he said he was following the footsteps of Nidal Hasan. He planned to blow up a restaurant when it was full of soldiers and shoot fleeing survivors. Abdo was acting strangely while buying material for an explosive device in a gun store, and an employee called the police. When he was arrested, he had a handgun, ammunition, and an Inspire Magazine article entitled, "Make a bomb in the kitchen of your Mom." He is serving two life sentences plus sixty years.

Bilal Abood

Bilal Abood was a translator for the U.S. military. Abood was convicted of lying to the FBI about his travels to Syria and allegiance to ISIL which he proclaimed on Twitter. Abood is serving a four-year prison sentence.

Jim David Adkisson

Adkisson was a veteran of the U.S. Army. He pled guilty to killing 2 people and injured another 6 at a Unitarian Universalist Church in Knoxville, Tennessee. He was motivated by hatred of Democrats, liberals, African Americans and homosexuals. Adkisson told investigators that he hoped to kill more and that all liberals should be killed. He is serving a life sentence in prison.

Hasan Akbar

Former Army Sgt. Hasan K. Akbar threw a grenade into a tent with sleeping soldiers from his brigade. He was convicted by court-martial of murdering two and attempted murder of sixteen other soldiers. Akbar was the first American soldier accused of killing fellow soldiers since the Vietnam War. He was sentenced to death and awaits execution.

Ryan Gibson Anderson

Anderson was a Specialist in the U.S. Army National Guard, where he was a tank crewman. He contacted al-Qaeda related websites and offered them U.S. military information. He was stripped of his grade and dishonorably discharged.

Jeffrey Leon Battle

Battle joined the U.S. Army Reserves to obtain training in U.S. tactics and weapons but failed basic training. Authorities say he intended to use his military experience against American soldiers in Afghanistan. Battle was part of the Portland Seven Terror Cell and was arrested for attempting to join al-Qaeda and the Taliban. At one time, Battle served as a bodyguard for Quanell X, a community activist and leader of the New Black Panthers. He pled guilty to conspiring to levy war against the U.S. and is serving an eighteen-year prison sentence.

Craig Benedict Baxam

Baxam joined the Army in 2007 as an Army intelligence specialist and expert in cryptology. He secretly converted to Islam after visiting radical websites. Within weeks after separating from the U.S. military, he was back in Maryland plotting his hijra — the obligatory migration to Islamic lands. He was arrested in Kenya where he attempted to join al

Shabaab. He is serving seven years in prison for attempting to provide support.

Joshua Cummings

Cummings was in the U.S. Army for five years, serving on a mortar squad. He was convicted of murdering a transit security guard in downtown Denver. He stated in an interview that he was committed to be a soldier for ISIS and swore allegiance to its leader, al-Baghdadi. Cummings said that he did not do the killing for ISIS, but only "for the pleasure of Allah." He is serving a life sentence in prison.

Hasan Edmonds

Edmonds was a Specialist stationed at the Joliet Armory. He was arrested for plotting an attack on the armory, having been caught surveying the base on FBI surveillance videos. Edmonds was sentenced to thirty years in prison for plotting the attack and attempting to fly overseas and fight for ISIS.

Daniel Seth Franey (Abu Dawuud)

Franey was in the U.S. Army for six years before he deserted. He allegedly told an undercover FBI agent that ISIS consisted of "the best people on Earth," that he would gladly leave his family and join ISIS, and that bin Laden was "a beautiful man," "a holy warrior," and "a diamond." He also, allegedly, wanted to behead police officers, and kill judges and the military. He is serving six years in prison for the unlawful possession of machine guns and other firearms.

Adam Nauveed Hayat

Hayat served as a machine gunner and military policeman in the U.S. Marines and took part in Operation Iraqi Freedom in 2004.

When he returned home, he became estranged from his family, homeless, and involved in the Occupy Wall Street movement. Hayat left pipe bombs in his Sheraton Hotel room in Denver, flying to California without paying his bill. He was arrested in a hotel in Los Angeles and eventually pled guilty to possession of unregistered explosive devices. The result of his August 2018, sentencing hearing was not known before this book went to press.

Robert Lorenzo Hester, Jr.

Hester was in the U.S. Army for less than a year before receiving a general discharge. An undercover FBI agent contacted Hester because of anti-government posts on social media. With the agent, Hester allegedly planned an attack on transportation services in Kansas City, and purchased materials to use in the attack. Hester also allegedly offered to provide firearms training, based on his military experience, to other participants in the attack. Hester awaits trial.

Kevin William Harpham

Harpham served in the U.S. Army at Fort Lewis, Washington. Harpham placed an explosive device along the Martin Luther King Jr. Day Unity March in Spokane, Washington, in 2011. The FBI found the bomb before the parade started. Thousands of message-board posts discussed dismantling or disrupting society. He is serving a thirty-two-year prison sentence for attempting to use a weapon of mass destruction and possession of an unregistered explosive device.

Eric Harroun

Harroun served in the U.S. Army for three years before he received a medical discharge. Harroun traveled first to Egypt, then to Syria and fought against the Syrian government with rebel groups that may have included al-Nasra and al-Nusra Front. He was charged with providing support to a terrorist organization and conspiring to use a weapon of mass destruction outside the U.S. but he pled guilty to conspiring to violate arms control laws. His sentence was time served (less than one year).

Nidal Hasan

Hasan is perhaps the most documented of the military men. Major Hasan was an Army psychiatrist stationed at Fort Hood, Texas. He went on a shooting spree, killing twelve of his fellow soldiers and a civilian, and wounding thirty-two others. He stated that anyone trying to stop the Taliban from establishing Sharia Law was an enemy of God and deserved to die. Hasan had communicated with Anwar al-Awlaki. He was sentenced to death and is awaiting execution.

Mohamed Bailor Jalloh

Jalloh was a member of the Virginia Army National Guard but allegedly decided not to re-enlist after listening to Awlaki online. Jalloh met with ISIL members during a trip to Nigeria and maintained communication with them. An undercover FBI employee facilitated the communication and help Jalloh plan an attack in the United States. Jalloh was arrested after he donated money through an undercover FBI employee and purchased an assault rifle from a Virginia gun dealer. Jalloh pled guilty to attempting to provide material support to ISIL. He is serving an eleven-year prison sentence.

Ikaika Erik Kang

Kang was a Sergeant First Class in the U.S. Army, stationed at Schofield Barracks, Hawaii, when he tried to transfer classified, military documents to ISIS. An FBI undercover agent began meeting with him after he became sympathetic to ISIS, watching propaganda videos online, and expressing interest in joining ISIS. Kang transferred Secret documents to the agent, provided military training, and swore an allegiance to ISIS. He is serving a twenty-five-year prison sentence after pleading guilty to attempting to provide material support to ISIS.

Allen Walter Lyon (Hammad Abdur-Raheem)

Lyon was an Army Sergeant who converted to Islam after serving a tour in the first Gulf War. He was also a member of the Virginia Jihad Cell, from which eleven members were convicted of crimes related to terrorism. Lyon served four years in prison for providing material support to a terrorist organization.

John Allen Muhammad

Muhammad, The DC Sniper, was a combat engineer in the Louisiana Army National Guard before transferring to the U.S. Army. He spent seventeen years in the military. Muhammad and a young accomplice killed ten and wounded three during a three-week sniping spree. He was convicted of murder with intent to terrorize the government or public, conspiracy to commit murder, and illegal use of a firearm. He converted to Islam twenty-years prior to the shootings and may have been a member of the Nation of Islam. He expressed sympathy with the 9/11 attacks and may have tried to extort ten million dollars from the U.S. government. Muhammad was executed in 2009.

Esteban Santiago

Santiago killed five people and injured six others in a mass shooting at the Fort Lauderdale-Hollywood International Airport in 2017. He is reported to be a decorated Army veteran of the Iraq

War and his service record includes the Army Reserves and the National Guard in Puerto Rico and Alaska. Some suggested his rampage was caused by post-traumatic stress disorder. Santiago had been treated for Schizophrenia, but he allegedly stated that his attack was in support of ISIS. He is serving five life sentences plus twenty-five years.

Roger Stockham

Stockham was arrested outside the Islamic Center of America in Dearborn, Michigan, with a car full of powerful fireworks. Authorities say he intended to attack the center during a funeral. He was a veteran of the U.S. Army and fought in the Vietnam War. Stockham had a history or threatening public buildings and officials, including President George W. Bush. He pleaded guilty by reason of being mentally ill and was released to a treatment center. He suffers from bipolar and post-traumatic stress disorders. Stokham has since been discharged.

Nicholas Michael Teausant

Teausant joined the U.S. Army National Guard but did not meet the requirements to continue and was in the process of being released when he was arrested. He expressed violent extremist ideology on social media and talked about bombing the Los Angeles subway system. Teausant was arrested while crossing into Canada with the intent of flying to the Middle East to join ISIS. He pled guilty to attempting to provide material support to ISIS and is serving a twelve-year prison sentence.

Brian Neal Vinas

Vinas joined the U.S. Army but did not finish boot camp. He was charged with receiving terrorist training, providing information to al-Qaeda, and conspiring to murder U.S. when he fired rockets at a U.S. Military base in Afghanistan. He cooperated with investigators for almost eight years after his arrest and provided valuable information about al-Qaeda. He was sentenced to time served plus three months.

Terrorists Who Served in the Marines

Theophilus Burroughs

Burroughs, who served in the Marines and was a high school music teacher, used his skills to sell military-grade weapons to undercover FBI agents who he thought represented Hamas. He was convicted of the criminal sale of firearms, tax fraud, money laundering, and conspiracy. He is serving a fifteen-year prison sentence.

Randall Blue Chapman (Seifuakllah)

Chapman served in the Marines until he received a medical discharged due to diabetes. Chapman became interested in Islam through his second wife, who was Muslim. He was one of the Virginia Jihad Cell members (aka the Paintball terrorists) and admitted to traveling to Pakistan and training with Lashkar-e-Tayyiba, but claimed it was not for jihad but for the grueling physical challenge. His conviction included charges relating to providing material support, criminal conspiracy, weapons violations, false statements, and plotting violence against friendly nations. Chapman was sentenced to eighty-five years in prison, but the judge later reduced it to sixty-five years. After serving fourteen years, Chapman's conviction was vacated and he was released because the use of "violence" in his charges was too vague, supported by a Supreme Court ruling in another case.

Clark Calloway

Calloway served as a Marine for four years and then became a construction worker. He was convicted of two felonies involving a stabbing after he left the military. The FBI investigated him after Calloway expressed support for ISIS and extreme racist ideologies on social media. He purchased and AK-47 automatic rifle and ammunition through an undercover FBI agent, allegedly saying that he wanted to use the gun on white people and a police station near his place of employment. In October 2018, he pled guilty to possession of a firearm by a felon and transport of a firearm with intent to commit a felony. He is awaiting sentencing.

Gregory Hubbard (Jibreel)

Hubbard was a fifty-four-year-old homeless man who served in the U.S. Marines. He was arrested in an FBI terrorism sting when he and two others tried to travel to Syria to fight with ISIS. He pled guilty to conspiring to provide material support to ISIS and prosecutors dropped two other charges related to the arrest. Hubbard is serving a twelve-year prison sentence.

Everett Aaron Jameson

Jameson graduated from basic training in the U.S. Marines with a rifle sharpshooter qualification; however, he was discharged for concealing his history of asthma. Jameson was a vocal supporter of ISIS and told undercover FBI agents that he was prepared to build and use explosives and to provide financial support to ISIS. He planned an ISIS-inspired, Christmas-Day attack on a popular local restaurant. He pled guilty to attempting to provide material support to ISIS and was sentenced to fifteen years in prison.

Matthew Aaron Llaneza

Llaneza served for a short time in the Marine Corps. His father indicated that he was discharged for an unknown reason. He described himself as proficient in weapons assembly and founded an internet sales and light manufacturing firm, Sand Fire Tactical. Llaneza chose to bring down a bank in Oakland, California, using a car bomb, with the help of an undercover FBI agent who claimed to be connected to the Taliban and mujahideen in Afghanistan. Llaneza parked what he thought was an explosive-laden vehicle near the bank in the middle of the night, armed the fake explosive device, and then used a cell phone to try and detonate it. He pleaded guilty to attempting to use a weapon of mass destruction, but because he tried to minimize casualties by attacking at night and has been diagnosed with schizophrenia, bipolar disorder, and post-traumatic stress disorder, the judge was lenient. Llaneza is serving a fifteen-year prison sentence.

Yonathan Melaku

Melaku is naturalized citizen from Ethiopia and a former Marine. He pled guilty to damaging property and firearms violations, having shot at the National Museum of the Marine Corps, the Pentagon, a Marine Corps recruiting sub-station, and a U.S. Coast Guard recruiting office. He was arrested at Arlington National Cemetery, where he intended to damage the grave markers of veterans who served in Iraq and Afghanistan. Melaku is serving a twenty-five-year prison sentence.

Donald T. Surratt

Surratt was a three-year veteran of the U.S. Marines, but was discharged after being shot in the leg during an armed robbery. Surratt allegedly began his conversion to Islam while serving in Somalia. He was one of eleven members of the Virginia Jihad Cell, a group of Muslim's who allegedly used paintball matches to train for jihad. The "Paintball Terrorists" were charged with thirty-two counts related to their plans to train with Lashkar-e-Tayyiba and then join al-Qaida and the Taliban to fight against U.S. troops. Surratt pled guilty to transporting weapons used in terrorist training and served two and one-half years of his 4-year prison sentence. He cooperated with authorities by testifying during the trials of his fellow paintballers.

Terrorists Who Served in the Navy

Joseph Anthony Davis (Abdul-Latif)

Davis served in the U.S. Navy but had a troubled life that included two suicide attempts, claims of hallucinations and hearing voices, criminal robbery and assault. He admired Osama bin Laden and condemned alleged atrocities committed by U.S. soldiers. The FBI began investigating him when he started broadcasting his extremist views. Davis and an accomplice purchased machine guns and planned to attack a military recruiting station in Seattle, Washington. An informant had arranged for faulty machine guns and the two were arrested when they took possession. He is serving an eighteen-year prison sentence

Paul Hall (Hassan Abu-Jihaad)

Hall was a Navy signalman. He revealed the location of Navy ships and their weaknesses online and discussed ship movements over the phone with a government informant. Hall was convicted of releasing previously classified information related to national defense. Hall served a ten-year prison sentence and was released in January 2016.

Kifah Jayyousi

Jayyousi is a naturalized citizen from Jordan who served in the U.S.

Navy and taught at Wayne State University, College of Engineering. Dr. Jayyousi is serving a twelve-year and eight-month prison sentence for conspiracy to murder, kidnap and maim overseas. He maintains his innocence. He published a newsletter that allegedly sensationalized the activities of the mujahedeen; he maintains that is was only slightly critical of U.S. policy. He raised money using two charities, American Islamic Group and American Worldwide Relief, and recruited soldiers in support of al-Qaeda related groups worldwide; he says it was charity work to benefit victims of the war in Bosnia and Chechnya.

Paul Gene Rockwood, Jr.

Rockwood served in the U.S. Navy and worked for the National Weather Service. After converting to Islam, Rockwood prescribed to the violent ideologies of Anwar Al-Awlaki. He felt a personal responsibility to exact revenge on anyone desecrating Islam. The FBI obtained a list of fifteen specific targets during their investigation and both Rockwood and his wife denied creating or knowing anything about the list. They later pled guilty to willfully making false statements to the FBI. Rockwood's wife was exiled to her native England while he served eight-years in prison. He was released in September 2017.

Zale H. Thompson (Zaim Farouq Abdul-Malik)

Thompson joined the Navy as a Builder Construction man's apprentice but was discharged two years later for misconduct. After earning a bachelor's degree and enrolling in a graduate program, Thompson converted to Islam and self-radicalized, frequenting hundreds of websites related to beheadings, al-Qaeda, ISIS, and al-Shabaab. Two years after his conversion he attacked four officers of the New York Police Department with a hatchet. One officer was critically injured, and another suffered minor injuries. Thompson was shot to death at the scene.

James W. Von Brunn

White Supremacist James W. Von Brunn commanded a PT boat in the U.S. Navy during the Pacific Theatre of World War II. After the leaving the Navy he was an advertising executive and producer in New York City. He also had a long criminal history including driving under the influence, fighting with a sheriff, attempted kidnapping, hostage taking, and burglary. He created an anti-Semitic website and wrote a book praising Adolf Hitler. On June 10, 2009, eighty-eight-year-old Brunn entered the U.S. Holocaust Memorial Museum in Washington, D.C. with a rifle and shot and killed a security guard. He was indicted on seven charges, but died of natural causes while awaiting a competency evaluation.

Terrorist Who Served in the U.S. Air Force

Tairod Nathan Webster Pugh

Pugh served the U.S. Air Force as an avionics instrument system specialist. He was trained to install and maintain aircraft engines, navigation systems, and weapons systems. Pugh was working as an aircraft mechanic in Kuwait when he traveled to Egypt and tried to enter Syria through Turkey to join ISIS, but officials in Turkey turned him away and he was deported back to the United States. He had proclaimed in a letter to his wife in Egypt that he planned to put his training to use for ISIS and would be victorious or become a martyr. He is serving a thirty-five-year prison sentence for attempting to provide material support to ISIS.

Terrorists Targeting the Military

It may be surprising that military veterans turn their back on the country they swore to defend and become terrorists, but it should not be surprising that the military is a terrorist target. They are, after all, the defenders of the U.S. government and the American way of life. Major Nidal Hasan and Joseph Davis targeted their own military bases, while Paul Hall shared the location and movements of Navy ships, making them terrorist targets. The following, with no military experience, targeted military installations for their terrorist acts.

Mohammad Abdulazeez

Abdulazeez killed four Marines and a Navy sailor in Tennessee at two military sites. He was born in Kuwait but moved to the U.S. with his family. Abdulazeez was conditionally hired as an engineer at the Perry nuclear power plant near Cleveland, Ohio, but was let go after ten days because he failed the background check.

Munir Abdulkader

Abdulkader's family is from Eritrea, in eastern Africa. U.S. officials say he was born there and became a naturalized U.S. citizen, but his mother swears he was born in the U.S. He was going to travel overseas and join ISIS, but received instructions from an ISIS leader to videotape the murder of a military based employee at his home and attack a police station in Cincinnati, Ohio. He was arrested when he tried to purchase an assault rifle for the attack. He pled guilty and is serving a twenty-year prison sentence.

Carlos Leon Bledsoe (Abdulhakim Mujahid Muhammad)

Bledsoe killed Private William Long and wounded Private Quinton Exeagwula in a drive-by shooting in front of the United States military recruiting office in Little Rock, Arkansas. Bledsoe faced twelve charges, including capital murder and unlawful discharge of a weapon. He pled guilty to everything but murder and was sentenced to life in prison.

Daniel Boyd

Daniel Boyd was the leader of the Raleigh Jihad Group which included his sons, Zakariya Boyd and Dylan Boyd. His father was a Marine, but Boyd was inspired by his stepfather to become Muslim. After high school he traveled to Pakistan and Afghanistan to join Islamic resistance fighters. Boyd and other members of his cell obtained a map of the base at Quantico with the plan to use armor-piercing bullets to kill the Americans.

James Cromitie / Newburgh Four Cell

Cromitie was part of the Newburgh Four cell, which plotted to blow up U.S. military planes at Stewart Air National Guard Base using Stinger missiles. The case was controversial, and the four defendants appealed their convictions based on entrapment; however, as pointed out in Chapter 3, the convictions were upheld by a U.S. Court of Appeals. Cromitie was a loudmouth Walmart employee who served jail time for drug convictions. He complained about the war in Afghanistan to a man at his Mosque, who turned out to be an FBI informant.

Comitie is serving a twenty-five-year prison sentence, the minimum sentence for one of the eighteen charges. The other members of the Newburgh Four include the following. David Williams served jail time from drug and weapon-related convictions prior to the terrorism-related offense. Onta Williams loaded trailers at a warehouse. Laguerre Payen served jail time for attempted assault prior to the terrorism-related offenses: he snatched purses from two women and shot people with a BB gun from a moving vehicle. During the trial, his lawyer said that he took medicine for Schizophrenia and had a very low, borderline IQ. The court found him competent. Relatives of each man said that they learned about Islam in prison. Cromitie, allegedly, recruited each of them.

Frederick Domingue Jr. (Walli Mujahidh)

Domingue and ex-military man, Joseph Anthony Davis (Abu Khalid Abdul-Latif) planned to attack a military recruiting center in Seattle, Washington. The plan consisted of the use of grenades and machine guns to slaughter military personnel and new recruits. An informant alerted authorities and the two were arrested when they tried to buy weapons for the attack. Domingue is serving a seventeen-year prison sentence after pleading guilty. Davis is serving eighteen years.

Marwan Othman El-Hindi

El-Hindi was one of three members of a Toledo Terror Cell. El-Hindi, Mohammad Zaki Amawi, and Wassim I. Mazloum planned to kill U.S. military personnel in Iraq. El-Hindi served thirteen years in prison and was released in May 2018. Amawi is serving a twenty-year sentence. Mazloam served eight-years and four- months and was released in April 2014.

Syed Hashmi

Hashmi was a graduate student living in London when he was arrested. He provided material support to al-Qaeda to help them fight U.S. soldiers in Afghanistan. His support included protective clothing and night vision goggles. Hashmi is serving a fifteen-year prison sentence.

Kevin James

James was the leader of the Torrance Four Terror Cell. The group began in Folsom State Prison and James named it Jam'yyat Al-Islam Al-Saheeh. They conspired to attack military targets in Los Angeles. He pled guilty to seditious conspiracy and was sentenced to sixteen years in prison. The other Torrence four members, that were also U.S. citizens including the following: Levar Haley Washington pled guilty to seditious conspiracy and was sentenced to twenty-two years. Gregory Vernon Patterson pled guilty to conspiring to levy war against the U.S. government through terrorism and was sentenced to twelve- and one-half years.

Antonio Martinez (Muhammad Hussain)

Martinez tried to blow up a military recruiting center outside of Boston, Massachusetts. Fortunately, he was discovered through social media posts and the car bomb that he used was a fake provided by an FBI informant. He pled guilty to attempting to use a weapon of mass destruction and was sentenced to twenty-five years in prison.

Abdirahman Sheik Mohamud

Mohamud received training on weapons, combat, and tactics in Syria, and then returned to the U.S. with a plan to attack a military base or a prison. His brother was Abdifatah Aden. Aden was killed fighting in Syria. Mohamud wanted to be like his brother, but after the death of his brother he returned to Ohio, just six weeks after arriving.

Mohamad Shnewer

Shnewer and four of his friends planned to kill soldiers at Fort Dix Army Base in New Jersey. They were supposed to hijack a gasoline truck, which Shnewer would drive into the military base. The group also discussed firing a rocket into the Philadelphia Naval Shipyard during the Army-Navy football game. Authorities were alerted to a video of the group shooting paintball guns and yelling "Allahu Akbar." An FBI informant foiled the plot. Shnewer was sentenced to life plus thirty years in prison.

Chapter Eleven Summary

This chapter presented the American terrorists who had military experience and who attacked military targets. Seeking a similar sense of brotherhood and feeling lost or alienated after separation were suggested as motivations for veterans to join or associate with terrorists organizations. On the other hand, training to become better killers may draw terrorists toward military service. Army soldiers appear to be the most susceptible to becoming terrorists. Alternatively, maybe the same personality is drawn to both the Army and terrorist organizations. Seven of these terrorists planned or executed acts related to terrorism while they were still serving in the military and thirty were no longer serving when they committed their crime. One was an employee of the military. Twenty-nine of the acts were violent.

Military installations and military service members are both in the top three terrorist targets. This makes sense since the goal of terrorism is to initiate change in the government or the public, and the military protects the government and the people of the United States of American.

Chapter Twelve

Behind Bars

Title 18 of the Federal Code defines "federal crime of terrorism" as an offense that is intended to influence or affect the conduct of government by intimidation or coercion, or retaliate against government conduct, and is a violation of certain sections of Title 18, which are listed in Table 9 (18 USC § 2332b(g)(5)).

The acts listed in Table 9 are crimes, regardless of their intent or purpose. The crimes become acts of terrorism when the perpetrator's goal in committing them to fulfill an ideological, religious, or political agenda. The prosecution normally has the burden of proving intent for specific crimes. In the case of terroristic crimes, the appearance of intent may be enough without any additional evidence (148).

Official Charges

This book uses the term "terrorist" to refer to people who have been charged with crimes that are related to terrorism. In reality, the majority of the terrorists are not charged with terrorism, but with infractions that have terroristic intent. The most frequent indictment among the American terrorists was providing material support to a terrorist or terrorist organization.

Seventeen of the charges are shown in Figure 31 and described in this chapter, along with the average prison sentence for the terrorists who were charged with each crime. Several crimes were not included in Figure 31 because there was only one instance, including bribery, smuggling, and counterfeiting. Court records and charges were readily available for three hundred twenty-seven of the American terrorists. The remaining were not available for various reasons including being at large, killed in battle, or awaiting a court hearing. Due to the variability of the term, life sentences were not included when calculating the average prison sentence.

The punishment handed down by a judge is influenced by several factors. The defendant is often tried on several indictments and the final sentence is based on the combination of charges for which the terrorist is convicted. In many cases, the defendant has agreed to a plea bargain, in which some of the charges are dropped if the defendant pleads guilty to one or several of the others. There are also cases in which one defendant agrees to cooperate during the prosecution of other defendants or by providing valuable information about terrorist activities. In those cases, the prosecution may recommend leniency in the sentencing.

1. Material Support

Nearly sixty percent of American terrorists were charged with providing material support. In American law, providing material support for terrorism is a crime prohibited by the USA PATRIOT Act (described in Chapter 13) and codified in Title 18 of the U.S. Code under Section 2339A, Providing Material Support to Terrorists; Section 2339B, Providing Material Support or Resources to Designated Foreign Terrorist Organizations; Section 2339C, Prohibitions against the Financing of Terrorism. The State Department designates terrorist organizations. The types of support can be property, services, monetary or financial securities, financial services, lodging, training, expert advice or assistance, safe-houses, false documentation or identification, communications equipment, facilities, weapons, lethal substances, explosives, personnel (may include self), or transportation. The jail sentence for providing support to terrorists is up to fifteen years, but the sentence can be up to twenty years for providing support to a terrorist organization.

For several of the terrorists, this was a standalone conviction.

Average Sentence Males: <u>15.6 Years</u>
Average Sentence Females: <u>9.0 Years</u>

2. Attempted Murder or Conspiracy to Kill

Criminal conspiracy is when two or more persons agree to commit an unlawful act at some time in the future. Attempted murder is the unsuccessful act of killing someone. Eighteen percent of the American terrorists charged with acts related to terrorism were in fact charged with conspiracy to kill or attempted murder. Title 18 covers murder, attempted murder, and conspiracy to kill with specific regard to terrorism in several sections. For example, section 930(c) specifically involves attacks on federal buildings, section 956(a)(1) applies when the target or victims is overseas, and in section 1114 the target is a U.S. officer or employee. Title 18, Chapter 51 is dedicated to homicide and covers it more broadly.

Average Sentence Males: <u>20.4 Years</u>
Average Sentence Females: <u>10.0 Years</u>

3. WMD / Bomb / Explosive Material

Fifteen percent of the terrorists were charged with a crime related to weapons of mass destruction (WMDs), bombs, or explosive materials. The violations include the use, threat of use, conspiracy to use, creation, storage, or the possession of the weapons or the materials used to make them. Title 18 covers these charges in several sections. Section 175 or 175b for biological weapons; 175c for variola virus; 229 for chemical weapons; 831 and 832 for nuclear material and 2332i for nuclear terrorism; 842(m) or (n) for plastic explosives; 2332a for the general use of weapons of mass destruction; 2332f for bombing of public places; and 844(i) for bombing of government property.

Average Sentence Males: <u>17.9 Years</u>
Average Sentence Females: <u>3.9 Years</u>

4. Making False Statements

Twelve and one-half percent of the American terrorists were charged with making false statements. Title 18 section 1001 prohibits knowingly and willfully making false or fraudulent statements or concealing information in "any matter within the jurisdiction" of the federal government of the United States. Several other sections deal with specific situations. For example, Section 1015 covers false statements relating to citizenship or registry of aliens.

Average Sentence Males: <u>11.8 Years</u>
Average Sentence Females: <u>9.5 Years</u>

5. Criminal Conspiracy

Twelve percent of American terrorists were charged with criminal conspiracy. As described above, criminal conspiracy is when two or more people agree to commit an unlawful act at some time in the future. Title 18, Chapter 19 is dedicated to conspiracy, and section 371 covers a general charge of conspiracy to commit offense or to defraud the United States.

Average Sentence Males: 13.1 Years
Average Sentence Females: 2.6 Years

6. Firearms Violations

Almost twelve percent of the American terrorists were charged with a firearm or other weapons violations. Title 18, Chapter 44 describes the unlawful acts related to firearms.

Average Sentence Males: 17.4 Years
Average Sentence Females: 1.25 Years

7. Immigration Violations

Nearly five percent of American terrorist were charged with immigration violations. These infractions are described in Title 18, Chapter 69, Nationality and Citizenship, as well as Title 8 which codifies the Immigration and Nationality Act.

Average Sentence Males: 8.5 Years

8. Money Laundering and Other Financial Violations

Just over four percent of American terrorists were charged with a financial violation, with money laundering being the most frequent. Title 18 Section 1956 relates to the laundering of monetary instruments, which refers to a financial transaction using the proceeds from an unlawful activity.

Average Sentence Males: <u>5.9 Years</u>
Average Sentence Females: <u>3.2 Years</u>

9. Terrorism

Nearly three percent of the American terrorists were actually charged with terrorism. Title 18 section 2332b covers acts of terrorism that occur in or outside the boarders of the U.S., and section 1992 covers terrorist attacks on mass transportation systems. In addition, three of the terrorists faced state charges of terrorism. Several states have analogs to 18 USC 2332b(a)(2) in their statutes.

Average Sentence Males: <u>7.7 Years</u>

10. Obstruction of Justice

Two and three-quarter percent of the American terrorists were charged with obstruction of justice, which is covered by Title 18 Sections 1501-1521. It means to willfully impede the communication of information that relates to any violation of a criminal statute of the United States.

Average Sentence Males: <u>6.7 Years</u>

11. Conspire to Levy War Against the United States

Close to two and one-half percent of American terrorists were charged with conspiring to levy war against the United States (see Figure 31). It is an act of treason and is the only crime listed in the Constitution. Title 18 Chapter 115 addresses treason, sedition, and subversive activities.

Average Sentence Males: <u>14.0 Years</u>
Average Sentence Females: <u>3.0 Years</u>

12. Receiving Military-Style Training from an International Terrorist Organization

Nearly two and one-half percent of American terrorists were charged with receiving military-style training from an international terrorist organization. This crime is outlined in Title 18 Section 2339D. The sentence is a fine or 10 years in prison or both. The accused must know that the organization has been designated as terrorist by the State Department or that the organization has engaged in terrorist activity.

Average Sentence Males: <u>18.3 Years</u>
Average Sentence Females: <u>4 Years</u>

13. Racketeering

One and two-tenths percent of the American terrorists were charged with racketeering. This crime is based on fraudulent business dealings which seek to extort money through violence or intimidation. Title 18, Chapter 96 discusses every aspect of racketeering.

Average Sentence Males: <u>6.4 Years</u>

14. Passport Fraud

One and two-tenths percent of the American terrorists were charged with passport fraud. Title 18, Chapter 75 deals with passports and visas.

Average Sentence Males: 15.0 <u>Years</u>
Average Sentence Females: <u>0.2 Years</u>

15. Plotting Violence Against Friendly Nations

One and two-tenths percent of the American terrorists were charged with plotting violence against a friendly nation. Title

18, Chapter 45 covers foreign relations, including Section 958, "Commission to serve against friendly nation," and Section 960, "Expedition against friendly nation."

Average Sentence Males: <u>25.1 Years</u>

16. Assault

Just under one percent of American terrorists were charged with assault. Section 2332b addresses assault in connection with an act of terrorism. The penalties can be up to 30 years, depending upon the circumstance. Additional sections of Title 18 deal with assaults on specific individuals, such as Section 1389 for assault against U.S. servicemen or their families, and Section 1751 covers assault of the President and staff.

Average Sentence Males: <u>9.0 Years</u>

17. Drug Violations

Less than one percent of the American terrorists were charged with drug violations. Many sections of Title 18 have drug offenses as compounding factors. The Controlled Substances Act outlines the criminal statutes with regard to drugs.

Average Sentence Males: <u>19.5 Years</u>

Federal Crimes Related to Terrorism from Title 18, U.S. Code, Chapter 113B

Section:	Related To:
32	Destruction of Aircraft or Aircraft Facilities
37	Violence at International Airports
81	Arson Within Special Maritime and Territorial Jurisdiction

175 or 175b	Biological Weapons
175c	Variola Virus
229	Chemical Weapons
351(a), (b), (c), (d)	Congressional Cabinet and Supreme Court Assassination and Kidnapping
831	Nuclear Materials
832	Participation in Nuclear and Weapons of Mass Destruction Threats to The U.S.
842(m) or (n)	Plastic Explosives
844(f)(2) or (3)	Arson and Bombing of Government Property Risking or Causing Death
844(i)	Arson and Bombing of Property Used in Interstate Commerce
930(c)	Killing or Attempted Killing During an Attack on A Federal Facility with A Dangerous Weapon
956(a)(1)	Conspiracy to Murder Kidnap or Maim Persons Abroad
1030(a)(1) and 1030(a)(5)(A)	Protection of Computers
1114	Killing or Attempted Killing of Officers and Employees of The United States
1116	Murder or Manslaughter of Foreign Officials, Official Guests or Internationally Protected Persons
1203	Hostage Taking
1361	Relating to Government Property or Contracts

1362	Destruction of Communication Lines Stations or Systems
1363	Injury to Buildings or Property Within Special Maritime and Territorial Jurisdiction of The United States
1366(a)	Destruction of an Energy Facility
1751(a), (b), (c), or (d)	Presidential and Presidential Staff Assassination and Kidnaping
1992	Terrorist Attacks and Other Acts of Violence Against Railroad Carriers and Mass Transportation Systems (Land, Water, or Air)
2155	Destruction of National Defense Materials, Premises or Utilities
2156	National Defense Materials, Premises, or Utilities
2280	Violence Against Maritime Navigation
2280a	Maritime Safety
2281 – 2281a	Violence Against Maritime Fixed Platforms
2332	Certain Homicides and Other Violence Against United States Nationals Occurring Outside of The United States
2332a	Use of Weapons of Mass Destruction
2332b	Acts of Terrorism Transcending National Boundaries
2332f	Bombing of Public Places and Facilities
2332g	Missile Systems Designated to Destroy Aircraft
2332h	Radiological Dispersal Devices
2332i	Nuclear Terrorism
2339	Harboring Terrorists
2339A	Providing Material Support to Terrorists

2339B	Providing Material Support to Terrorist Organizations
2339C	Financing of Terrorism
2338D	Military-Type Training from a Foreign Terrorist Organization
2340A	Torture

Table 9: Federal Crimes of terrorism according to Title 18, U.S. Code, Chapter 113B, § 2332b(g)(5).

FBI Involvement

Catching a terrorist before he or she commits the act can be quite difficult. The Federal Bureau of Investigation (FBI) has lead-agency responsibility for investigating acts of terrorism. Typically, the FBI receives a tip from someone who sees radical beliefs expressed on social media or other public forum. If an investigation reveals genuine potential for terroristic activity, an undercover agent or FBI informant may attempt to befriend the person of interest. The FBI will then arrange a sting in which the potential terrorists will have the opportunity to act upon the extremist views they expressed. Some of the American terrorists claimed that the FBI entrapped them; however, if the person shows a predisposition toward perpetrating the crime, ultimately chooses the crime and the target, and takes steps toward accomplishing the infraction, then they were not entrapped, they were caught. The FBI helped to prevent American terrorists from completing their goals in sixty-four percent of the cases (see Figure 30).

FBI Involvement

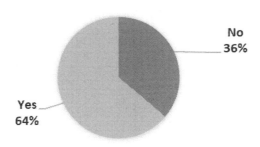

Figure 30: The FBI has thwarted many terrorist attacks and has been involved in sixty-four percent of the investigations and arrests of American terrorists since 9/11.

Prison Location

U.S. citizens charged with acts related to terrorism are serving jail time in at least twenty-eight different prisons across the U.S. (see Figures 31). The location of incarceration was not available for all the terrorists on our list. Some were still awaiting trial or sentencing, and some have already served their full prison sentence. Others were still fugitives, killed, or committed suicide.

Pennsylvania holds the greatest number of American terrorists, followed by New York, Colorado, and Illinois (see Figures 31 & 32).

It is interesting to note that four hundred eighteen of the American terrorists lived in twenty-four of the states in which terrorists were imprisoned. Are the terrorists being placed near their pre-incarceration homes, or do would-be terrorists intentionally move to states with prisons holding other terrorists? In other words, do American citizens with a desire to carry out terrorist attacks make an effort to live near their perceived heroes?

Figure 31: U.S. map showing the number of American terrorists held in prisons in each state. The shade of orange darkens with the increasing number of terrorists.

Sentencing

Males on average receive a longer sentence than females even if the charges are similar (see Figures 33 and 35). The average sentence applied to males was just over thirteen years, while the average for females was just over eight years. As discussed in Chapter nine, there is a long-standing gender gap related to sentences and sentence length. For this study the women received an approximate twenty-five percent reduced sentence compared to their male counterparts. When this calculation was done in 2015 (during the collection of data for this book), the gap was much larger, nearly fifty percent. This leads us to believe the judicial system has begun to regard the females as terrorists themselves, and not as victims. Not all of the American terrorists are included in the sentencing statistics. (See Figure 34) Reasons for exclusion include the following: Life sentences were handed to twenty of the men, while seventeen of them were still waiting for their trial or sentencing. The list also includes three suicides, seven killed during arrest, two killed in a drone strike, three who died before sentencing, and two who were given a death sentence. Five remain as fugitives.

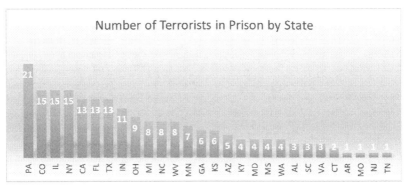

Figure 32: The number of terrorists held in prisons in the indicated states as of January 2018.

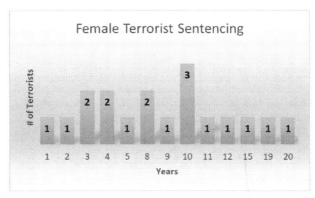

Figure 33: The number American females sentenced to each of the indicated years in prison for acts related to terrorism. The average jail sentence for females was 8.3 years.

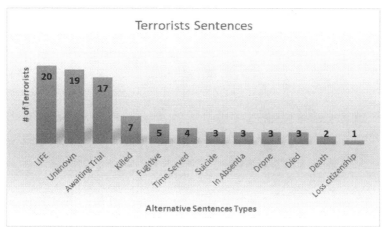

Figure 34: The number of American terrorists with the indicated alternative sentences or fates, which cannot be categorized by the number of years of imprisonment.

The Targets of American Terrorists

The chance of an average American being the focus of a terror attack is slim. Figure 36 reveals the top targets of American terrorists. Military personnel and military installations are both in the top three, with a combined forty-two terrorists targeting them. Public places are second on the list, having been the object of destruction by twenty-two terrorists.

The list of top targets include bridges at #5, with eleven terrorists choosing bridges choosing them as their target, including one cell in Ohio, one cell in New York, and two independent operatives. Khalid Sheikh Mohammed, the principal architect of the 9/11 attacks told his interrogators at Guantanamo Bay that Iyman Faris' target was the one hundred sixteen-year-old Brooklyn Bridge. He decided that the bridge was too difficult to target. In Cleveland, Ohio, the FBI thwarted the deadly plans of the Revolutionary People's Group: Douglas Wright, Brandon Baxter, Anthony Hayne, Joshua Stafford, and Connor Stevens.

The young men tried to detonate C4-plastic explosives that they had attached to a bridge, but the bomb was inert, compliments of the FBI.

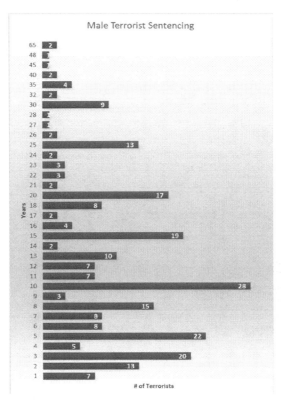

Figure 35: The number of American males convicted of acts related to terrorism and their sentence lengths.

Emerson Winfield Begolly established the Ansar al-Mujahideen English Forum (AMEF), an Islamic extremist web forum to promote jihad and encouraged readers to attack bridges, military facilities, and police stations, among other things. He posted instructions for making a bomb and was eventually charged with solicitation to commit a crime of violence and distribution of information relating to explosives.

Munther Omar Saleh and the ISIS New York Cell plotted to blow up the George Washington Bridge between New York and New Jersey. Authorities observed him surveying the bridge and the FBI monitored his efforts to procure bomb making supplies.

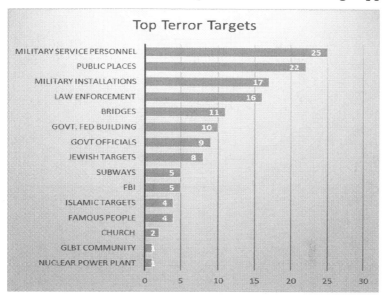

Figure 36: The number of American terrorists whose crimes involved the indicated targets. Military personnel and installations are both in the top three. Public places include malls, outdoor events, and other places of gathering.

Crimes Involving Violence

Terrorism is typically a violent crime, by default. It generates notions of fanatics who are intent on killing crowds of people. The activities of three hundred eighteen American terrorists were categorized as violent or non-violent. The remainder were missing information that was important for categorizing. In line with expectations, seventy-one percent of the terroristic activities involved violence (see Figure 37).

185

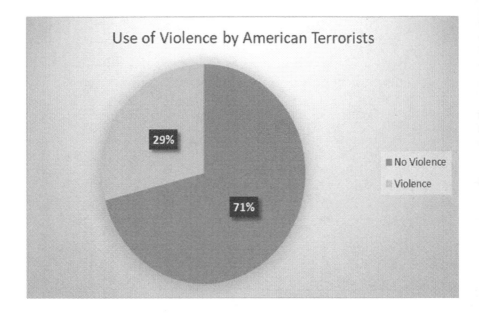

Figure 37: The distribution of violent and non-violent crimes among those Americans arrested for crimes related to terrorism.

Weapons Used

The majority of crimes committed by American males and females charged with acts related to terrorism did not involve weapons (see Figure 38). The most common weapon is in line with our expectations when we think of terrorists: explosives.

Two American-born terrorists, Andrew Stack and Charles Bishop, used aircraft as their weapons of choice. Andrew Joseph Stack III, a computer engineer who was against government, big business, and taxes, smashed a small aircraft into an IRS center in a Texas office building. Stack and an IRS manager were killed, and thirteen others were injured. Charles Bishop, the youngest terrorist on the list at age fifteen, and aligned with al-Qaeda, flew a small plane into a skyscraper in Florida, killing only himself.

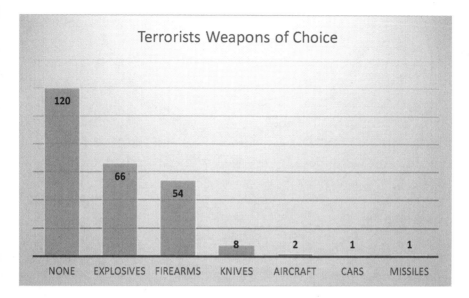

Figure 38: The number of American terrorists who used or intended to use the weapons indicated. Explosives include bombs and grenades. Firearms include rifles and hand guns.

Recidivism

Recidivism is the tendency of a convicted criminal to re-offend. For terrorists, it refers to the process by which a disengaged terrorist reengages or re-offends (149). Research on recidivism in terrorists is lacking (150); however, incidents in Paris, London, and Sydney involved individuals with a history of criminal activity (151), suggesting that there is a potential for recidivism among terrorists. Jihadists, however, are not released from prison very often, and so recidivism trends are difficult to analyze (149,152). Prediction models for other types of violence have not proven useful for terrorism (153).

Great concern was generated around the release of detainees at Guantanamo Bay and the threat they pose. New research suggests that up to twenty-eight percent of former detainees had reengaged in terrorism (151,154). As the prison sentences of the American terrorists mature, there should be a process by which their viewpoints on religion, politics, and government are evaluated and recorded. Along with prison time, offenders are sentenced to a period of monitoring after they are released. Their attitudes should be evaluated during that period also in order to track changes that lead to productive life versus re-radicalization.

Shaker Masri attempted to travel from his home in Chicago, Illinois, to Somalia to join al Shabaab. It was August of 2010 and he was twenty-six years old. Masri made plans for the trip with an associate who turned out to be a cooperating source working with the FBI. Masri pleaded guilty in July 2012 to conspiring to provide material support to a designated foreign terrorist organization (al-Shabaab), a violation of 18 CFR § 2339B, which has a maximum penalty of twenty years in prison. His plea agreement gave him a prison sentence of nine years and ten months, followed by twenty years of monitoring. Marsi was released in February 2018, admitting that his actions were juvenile and irresponsible. He claimed that there was no exit interview and no risk assessment when he was released. No one in prison had tried to understand what drew him to jihadist ideology or if he was still inclined to follow the same beliefs (155).

Thirty-one percent of the American terrorists were arrested before 2009; more than ten years ago at the publishing of this book. Some convicted terrorists have already completed their prison sentence, and more will be released as time progresses. Will they be responsible, contributing citizens, or will they feel angry and alienated, and end up repeating the cycle? Perhaps reaching their goals the second time around.

Deradicalization

The data on the success of deradicalization programs is also severely lacking. It can be difficult to obtain permission to interview prisoners and learn about their inspiration, the process by which they were radicalized, and their current state of radicalization (151).

There are several deradicalization programs outside of the U.S. that were implemented with the hope of reducing terrorist recidivism. These programs combine psychology, counseling, employment, housing, and education with the hope of improving long-term success (150,151). Andrew Silke, a professor at Cranfield University, UK, suggests that disengagement is more effective than deradicalization (156). Silke cites successful, historic disengagement programs in Italy and Spain and suggests that their success stems from not trying to change beliefs. Instead, they aimed to help non-violent offenders, who had largely already decided not to continue the terrorist life, to reintegrate into society. Disengagement involves cutting all connections to terrorist networks. Those arrested for terrorist offenses must renounce violence as a means to achieving their goals. Since the programs are for non-violent offenders, it is no surprise that most of them have already made that decision.

Seventy-one percent of the crimes committed were nonviolent. This leads the authors to believe that the use of deradicalization programs that resemble disengagement should prevent recidivism in the American terrorists. Moreover, a disengagement program that shields people from extremist ideas in favor of social integration may prevent radicalization in the first place.

Chapter Twelve Summary

The federal crime of terrorism is an offense intended to influence or affect the conduct of the government by intimidation or coercion, or to retaliate against government conduct. Since the terrorists discussed in this book are U.S. citizens, they have committed crimes against their country. The most frequent offense involved providing material support to terrorists or terrorist organizations. The average prison sentence for men who were charged with material support was about fifteen and one-half years, while their overall average for all terror-related crimes was about thirteen years. Females accused of material support had sentences averaging nine years, while their overall average was about eight years. Given that seventy one percent of the crimes were violent, it is no surprise that the next two most common charges were attempted murder or conspiracy to kill and crimes involving weapons of mass destruction, bombs, and explosive materials.

The state of Pennsylvania was revealed to hold the most prisoners charged with crimes related to terrorism. It holds forty percent more than the next highest states, Colorado, Illinois, and New York. Twenty-eight different states have American terrorists in their prisons. Arkansas, Missouri, New Jersey, and Tennessee have the fewest, holding one prisoner each.

Men typically receive a longer prison sentence than women. This is true, historically, whether the case is related to terrorism; however, over time, the average prison sentence for women charge with acts of terrorism has gotten closer to that for men. We suggest that this signals recognition that women can be terrorists of their own choosing and should receive punishments on equal par with their male counterparts.

The targets of terroristic activity are not surprising. Five of the top seven targets include military personnel and property, law enforcement, and government buildings and officials. These marks are integral to the objectives of many terrorists: to affect the policies or operation of the government. The other two in the top seven are public places and bridges, which represent another aspect of terrorism: intimidation of the public in order to advance their objectives. It is interesting to note that most of the crimes did not involve weapons; however, material support was the most common offense, and that may involve sending money or materials or one's self to terrorist organizations, for which weapons are not necessary.

The most surprising revelation in this chapter is how little we know about life after prison for the American terrorists. Recidivism seems likely for some, but there appears to be no organized effort to track and/or prevent such occurrence. Should prisoners undergo deradicalization, by which they are convinced not to pursue radical beliefs? Would a disengagement process be more successful, by which non-violent offenders can renounce the use of violence to support their beliefs, reduce their sentences, and reintegrate into society? Perhaps a combination of both approaches would work best; however, recruitment by extremists also occurs in prison. Successfully reducing the number of American terrorists might require curbing radicalization within the prisons as well as recidivism post-incarceration.

Chapter Thirteen

Prevention Strategies and Federal Policies

One way to stop terrorism is to prevent the recruitment of our young men, and in ten percent of the cases, women. Another is to prove terrorism is ineffective as a tactic to achieve their political, religious or ideological goals (157). We need to offer an alternative that appeals to pre-radicalized individuals. In Chapter 10 the profile of a terrorist was outlined. When the profile is used to recognize a developing terrorist in your neighborhood, workplace, or school, the path to extremism can be diverted. Lessening the appeal of terrorism is the first step to reducing extremism (158). One way is by deconstructing the fabrications terrorist organizations use for recruiting new members (Ibid). Particularly materials shared on social media.

The Use of the Terrorist Profile as a Tool for Prevention

A potential terrorist may not match all of the elements of the profile presented in Chapter Ten, but by identifying those who fit much of the profile, the likelihood of diverting some potential terrorists away from radicalization is increased. Fixed elements such as gender and age help to narrow the population of interest. Knowing economic class and education level further delineates the chance of radicalization and increases the probability of correctly identifying someone in need of help.

The individual may feel alone, not having a girlfriend or wife, and possible not many friends. Teachers, coaches, family members, or friends can help the individual feel that someone cares, that they are not alone. The condition is compounded when the person is raised without a father figure. There are organizations that provide role models to help guide young people toward success in life, like Big Brothers Big Sisters of America. Elders in the neighborhood, in places of worship, or in schools, are happy to fill such roles.

Our idea of home can have a strong influence on our psychological welfare. When removed from the security or comfort of home, people can feel out of place and begin to look for ways to fit into their new environment. They become open to ideas they would normally resist and may succumb to extremist ideas. Home may be another country or state, or a new environment: rural versus urban for example. We can help displaced people acclimate to their new surroundings by getting them involved in the community, teaching them about the local culture, learning about their culture and helping to find similarities in their new location.

The angry or victimized person is ripe for recruitment by radical groups. Extremism is born of anger: the extreme views or actions provide an outlet for anger and give the person a target for their blame. The anger can stem from many experiences such as a history of trauma or stress, experiencing humiliation or shaming in school or at home. Anger can provide a sense of power to someone who feels powerless. Anger can also stem from a narrow view of life that places unrealistic barriers on a person's potential. A person struggling to find employment may also experience anger. These individuals need alternative outlets for their anger and guidance to help them see a path for their success. Public services for employment or job searching have become common place, but sometimes a person needs help to take advantage of the services available. Anger itself can also be managed. In Australia, terror suspects are required to take anger management classes and counseling to turn them from violence (159).

De-radicalization and Disengagement

One approach to counter terrorism is the creation of de-radicalization programs (160). Saudi Arabia was one of the first to be so innovative (161). The success of de-radicalization programs is still in question. A released Guantanamo prisoner enrolled in the Saudi program in 2006 but joined AQAP two years later (158).

In 2016, the first radicalization program in the U.S. was started in Minnesota, which included four ISIS recruits. Daniel Koehler, director of the German Institute on Radicalization and De-radicalization Studies, trained the leaders of the program. The first step was to conduct risk assessments and create a personal deradicalizing plan. U.S. probation and pretrial officers were trained to supervise the defendants. Officials hoped this plan would provide a template for future programs, but its success is still being evaluated. Not every radicalized individual will respond to the counseling, and some will take much longer than others.

American citizen, Jesse Morton, was known as Younus Abdullah Muhammad when he recruited for al-Qaeda. He founded "Revolution Muslim," a website that published radical content encouraging violent jihad against non-Islamic worshipers. While in prison for acts related to terrorism, Morton worked undercover and assisted in counter-terrorism efforts. He believes the undercover work added in his deradicalization.

By abandoning the violence and any involvement with other terror members, a radicalized person can leave the lifestyle without changing their life views (157). The fear of persecution by the law may force a radicalized individual to back away from violet action, but they still recruit or spread propaganda (Ibid). Prevention of radicalization for vulnerable youth, prison inmates, gang members, and military means separation from radical ideas and providing activities that steer them away from violence and into non-violent solutions (Ibid).

Federal Policies Related to Terrorism

President Obama wrote policy standards and procedures that formalized and strengthened the process for capturing or killing a terrorist. President Trump's directives aim to limit the entry of refugees and immigrants and tighten the vetting process. The responsibility for preventing terrorism, however, falls mainly upon the Department of Homeland Security (DHS). President George W. Bush proposed the creation of DHS, and Congress approved it with the Homeland Security Act of 2002. A great deal of money, about $2.8 trillion from 2002 to 2017 (163), and resources have been dedicated to protecting the nation and its citizens from terrorism, through the DHS and other agencies. During the year following 9/11, forty-eight anti-terrorism bills and resolutions were approved or signed into law, including the USA Patriot Act, which is described later in the chapter. In fact, ever major terrorist event seems to be followed by an onslaught of legislation. In 2015 and 2016, when ISIS was rapidly growing, thirty pieces of terror-related legislation were enacted. Terrorism did not start with 9/11, as we have already pointed out. Several important laws and executive orders were also enacted prior to al-Qaeda's major offensive.

The Biological Weapons Anti-Terrorism Act of 1989 (BWATA)

Passed in 1990 and amended in 1996, the BWATA defined and outlawed biological warfare. The buying, selling, illegitimate use, and possession of biological weapons were made illegal. The Centers for Disease Control and Prevention was tasked to establish a regulatory regime to monitor biological agents (164). The BWATA and its amendment accomplished the following.

- Amended the Federal criminal code to make it a crime to develop, produce, stockpile, transfer, acquire, retain, or possess any biological agent, toxin, or delivery system that will be used or assist the use as a weapon.

- Provided for Federal jurisdiction outside of the U.S. over an offense committed by or against a U.S. national.

- Authorized the Attorney General to request a warrant authorizing the seizure of any bio-agent, toxin, or delivery system that has no apparent permissible use and without a warrant in urgent circumstances.

• Authorized the United States to obtain a ruling against conduct prohibited by this Act.

• Authorizes the interception of wire, oral, or electronic communications related to biological weapons offenses under specified conditions.

Executive Order 12947

Prohibiting Transactions with Terrorists Who Threaten to Disrupt the Middle East Peace Process.

President Clinton believed the acts of foreign terrorists were a threat to National Security and declared a national emergency. He published Executive Order 12947, which made it a crime to sponsor or provide financial, material, or technological support to terrorist organizations (165). The Order demanded the following.

• All property and interests in property of foreign people involved in terrorist acts be blocked

• Anyone assisting in, sponsoring, or providing financial, material, or technological support for, or services in support of, in the United States or within the possession or control of a United States person, is blocked.

• Any transaction or dealing by U.S. citizens, or within the United States related to terrorism are prohibited, including funds, goods, or services, and donations.

• Any investigation shall first be coordinated with the Federal Bureau of Investigation (FBI). The FBI shall timely notify the Department of the Treasury of any action it takes on such referrals.

Omnibus Counter-terrorism Act of 1995

The Omnibus act preceded the Patriot Act. Its highlights include allowing indictments based on secret evidence, making terrorism a new federal crime, allowing use of the U.S. military for civilian law enforcement, and allowing permanent detention of non-U. S. citizens. The Act was intended to do the following.

- Provide Federal law enforcement with the necessary tools to address acts of international terrorism occurring in the U.S. or directed against the U.S. and its people.

- Prevent persons and organizations from providing funds to organizations, including subordinate or affiliated persons engaging in terrorism.

- Provide procedures allowing the government to deport resident and non-resident alien terrorists promptly, without compromising intelligence sources.

- Provide Federal law enforcement the necessary tools to combat the threat of nuclear contamination and proliferation.

- Implement the Convention on the Marking of Plastic Explosives for the Purpose of Detection, which occurred in Montreal on 1 March 1991.

U.S. Antiterrorism and Effective Death Penalty Act of 1996 (AEDPA)

The AEDPA sought to deter terrorism, provide justice for victims, and provide for an effective death penalty. Its provisions included the following.

- Provided restitution and assistance for victims of terrorism.

- Identified foreign terrorist organizations.

- Placed restrictions on nuclear, biological, or chemical weapons.

Executive Order 13224 (2001)

President George W. Bush issued the Order on September 23, 2001, in response to the attacks on 9/11. It authorized the U.S. Treasure to disrupt the financial-support network for terrorists and terrorist organizations by blocking the assets of individuals supporting terrorist and terrorist organizations.

USA PATRIOT Act and the USA Freedom Act

The Uniting and Strengthening America by Providing Appropriate Tools for Intercepting and Obstructing Terrorism Act (USA PATRIOT Act) was enacted just 40 days after the 9/11 attack that destroyed the twin towers in New York City. It was amended in March 2006.

This act was created to deter and punish terrorist acts in the United States. It authorized new powers for the Federal Government and improved the tools available to law enforcement. The PATRIOT Act created new crimes, penalties, and procedural efficiencies for use against domestic and international terrorists. It was controversial because many believed it infringed on the civil liberties of U.S. citizens. Furthermore, the PATRIOT Act allowed the indefinite detention of non-citizens without probable cause. The law expired in 2011 but was extended by President Obama for an additional four years. It was replaced by the USA Freedom Act in 2015, which extended the essential provisions of the USA PATRIOT Act but offered greater transparency. The act provides the following.

- Allows investigators to use the same tools currently used in non-terrorism crimes, such as drug crimes and mail and passport fraud, to fight terrorism.

- Allows wiretaps to investigate some of the crimes related to terrorism.

- Enables investigators to gather certain information to prosecute terrorism-related offenses, such as weapons of mass destruction, terrorism financing, and the killing Americans abroad.

- Allows federal agents to use a "roving wiretap," which focuses on an individual rather than a phone.

- Allows law enforcement to use Delayed Notification Search Warrants when investigating terrorism, which prevents advance notice to the person of interest.

- Allows federal agents to obtain business records in national security terrorism cases.

- Facilitates information sharing and collaboration among government agencies by removing legal barriers that prevented the law enforcement, intelligence, and national defense communities from working together.

- Updates the law to reflect advanced technologies and threats so that the process for obtaining a search warrant is streamlined and effective across jurisdictions.

- Allows victims of computer hacking to seek law enforcement assistance to combat the hackers.

- Increases the number of terroristic criminal offenses, their penalties, and their statute of limitations.

- The Lone Wolf Amendment categorizes individuals (non-U.S. citizens) as terrorists even if they are not affiliated with a known terrorist organization.

Homeland Security Act of 2002, Pub. L. 107-296

The Homeland Security Act consolidated twenty-two federal agencies and bureaus into the Department of Homeland Security (DHS). The DHS has a mandate to prevent and respond to natural and man-made disasters.

Border Protection, Anti-terrorism, and Illegal Immigration Control Act of 2005 (Sensenbrenner Bill)

The Sensenbrenner Bill sought to increase protection of U.S. borders through strengthened enforcement of immigration law and improved boarder security.

Detainee Treatment Act of 2005 (H.R. 2863, Title X)

This act made it implicitly illegal to torture Guantanamo detainees. Torture was defined as "cruel, inhuman, or degrading treatment or punishment." It also provided "uniform standards" to be used when interrogating detainees, who could no longer challenge the legality of their detention in federal court.

Military Commissions Act of 2006 (HR-6166, MCA)

President Bush signed the MCA into law in 2006. It authorized the trial of detained terrorism suspects by military commission, justified by terrorism being an act of war. It is controversial because some believe it denies Due Process and other believe it violates the Geneva Convention.

Chapter Thirteen Summary

This chapter introduced some of the key legislation that came about to combat terrorism. There is no doubt that these changes were necessary for the protection of U.S. citizens and the country from terrorism. Crimes related to terrorism are particularly foreboding because they have the potential for causing great property damage and a high death toll by appalling methods. In order to prevent violent terrorist attacks, it is necessary to aggressively seek out would be terrorists and prevent them from executing acts of terror. It is certain that more attacks would have occurred inside the U.S. if law enforcement were not adept at investigating and averting terrorism.

Deradicalization was discussed further as a way to divert certain individuals out of the prison system and back into society. The success of such programs seems specific to individuals. Those with a desire to separate from radical ideas and influences will find help in such programs, but other will meet with little success. In this way, both paths must be pursued: stiff penalties for those with low hope of disengaging from violence, and deradicalization for those who are likely to embrace peaceful methods to achieve their goals.

The chapter also clarified the profiling idea that each chapter has mentioned. By recognizing the characteristics most common in those who have become American terrorists, we can be on the lookout for individuals who might be vulnerable to radicalization.

Then we can offer help that might show them a better path and prevent their radicalization. By altering their path, we can eliminate the very attributes which terrorist recruiters use to identify potential targets.

References

(1) Federal Bureau of Investigation. Terrorism 2002-2005. 2016.

(2) Federal Bureau of Investigation. What We investigate, Terrorism, Definitions. 2018.

(3) Department of Defense. JP 1-02, Department of Defense Dictionary of Military and Associated Terms. 2018.

(4) Federal Bureau of investigation. Hate Crime Definition. 2016.

(5) Jackson SA. Domestic Terrorism in the Islamic Legal Tradition. the Muslim World 2001;91(3/4):293.

(6) Hoffman B. "Holy Terror": The Implications of Terrorism Motivated by A Religious Imperative. Studies in Conflict & Terrorism 1995;18(4):271-284.

(7) United States Department of State. Foreign Terrorist Organizations. 2018.

(8) Smith BL. Terrorism in America: Pipe Bombs and Pipe Dreams. SUNY Press; 1994.

(9) Nacos BL. Terrorism and Counterterrorism. 5th Ed. New York: Routledge; 2016.

(10) Lafree G, Dugan L. introducing the Global Terrorism Database. Terrorism and Political Violence 2007; 19:181.

(11) Kroessler JA. Bombing for Justice: Urban Terrorism in New York City from the 1960s Through the 1980s. Criminal Justice and Law Enforcement Annual 2014; 6:63.

(12) Iadicola P, Shupe A. Violence, inequality, and Human Freedom. Rowman & Littlefield; 2012.

(13) Saney I. Cuba: A Revolution in Motion. Fernwood Pub.; 2004.

(14) Landau AK, Smith WS. Keeping Things in Perspective: Cuba and the Question of international Terrorism. Center for international Policy Washington, DC; 2001.

(15) Joosse P. Leaderless Resistance and Ideological inclusion: The Case of the Earth Liberation Front. Terrorism and Political Violence 2007;19(3):351-368.

(16) Leader SH, Probst P. the Earth Liberation Front and Environmental Terrorism. Terrorism and Political Violence 2003;15(4):37-58.

(17) Lewis JE. Testimony Before the Senate Judiciary Committee, Washington DC, May 18, 2004, John E. Lewis, Deputy Assistant Director, Federal Bureau of investigation. 2004.

(18) Feuer A. Antifa On Trial: How A College Professor Joined the Left's Radical Ranks, Rolling Stone. 2018.

(19) Pridemore WA, Freilich JD. The Impact of State Laws Protecting Abortion Clinics and Reproductive Rights on Crimes Against Abortion Providers: Deterrence, Backlash, Or Neither? Law Hum Behav 2007;31(6):611-627.

(20) Altum JC. Anti-Abortion Extremism: The Army of God. Chrestomathy: Annual Review of Undergraduate Research at the College of Charleston 2003;'2:1-12.

(21) Schaff E. Redefining Violence Against Women: The Campaign of Violence and the Delay of RU486. Temp.Pol.& Civ. Rts.L.Rev. 1998;8:311.

(22) Monagle K. How We Got Here. Peace Review 1995;7(3-4):377-382.

(23) Jefferis J. Armed for Life: The Army of God and Anti-Abortion Terror in the United States: the Army of God and Anti-Abortion Terror in the United States. ABC-CLIO; 2011.

(24) Smith AG. The Implicit Motives of Terrorist Groups: How the Needs for Affiliation and Power Translate into Death and Destruction. Polit Psychol 2008;29(1):55-75.

(25) Mason C. Who's Afraid of Virginia Dare-Confronting Anti-Abortion Terrorism After 9/11. U.Pa.J.Const.L. 2003;6:796.

(26) Balch RW. The Rise and Fall of Aryan Nations: A Resource Mobilization Perspective. Journal of Political and Military Sociology 2006;34(1):81.

(27) Zeskind L. the" Christian Identity" Movement: Analyzing Its theological Rationalization For Racist and Anti-Semitic Violence. Division of Church and Society of the National Council of the Churches of Christ in the USA; 1987.

(28) Lule J. News Strategies and the Death of Huey Newton. Journalism & Mass Communication Quarterly 1993;70(2):287-299.

(29) Pearson H. The Shadow of the Panther: Huey Newton and the Price of Black Power in America. Da Capo Press; 1995.

(30) Umoja AO. Repression Breeds Resistance: The Black Liberation Army and the Radical Legacy of the Black Panther Party. New Political Science 1999;21(2):131-155.

(31) Heynen N. Bending the Bars of Empire from Every Ghetto for Survival: the Black Panther Party's Radical Antihunger Politics of Social Reproduction and Scale. Ann Assoc Am Geogr 2009;99(2):406-422.

(32) Joseph PE. Black Liberation Without Apology: Recon-

ceptualizing the Black Power Movement. the Black Scholar 2001;31(3-4):2-19.

(33) Rosenau W. "Our Backs Are Against the Wall", the Black Liberation Army and Domestic Terrorism in 1970s America. Studies in Conflict & Terrorism 2013;36(2):176-192.

(34) Stern J. the Covenant, the Sword, and the Arm of the Lord. Toxic Terror. Cambridge: MIT Press, 2000.

(35) Pickering LJ. The Earth Liberation Front, 1997-2002. PM Press; 2007.

(36) Kahane M, Kahane BZ. Never Again. 1971.

(37) Dershowitz AM. the Best Defense. Vintage, 2011.

(38) Klan KK. Ku Klux Klan.; 1927.

(39) Baker K. Gospel According to the Klan: the KKK's Appeal to Protestant America, 1915-1930. JSTOR; 2011.

(40) Perlmutter P. Legacy of Hate: A Short History of Ethnic, Religious, and Racial Prejudice in America. ME Sharpe; 1999.

(41) Klein AG. A Space for Hate: The White Power Movement's Adaptation into Cyberspace. Litwin Books Sacramento, CA; 2010.

(42) Mattias Gardell. Gods of the Blood: The Pagan Revival and White Separatism. Duke University Press; 2003.

(43) Perry B. "Button-Down Terror": The Metamorphosis of the Hate Movement. Sociological Focus 2000;33(2):113-131.

(44) Turk AT. Sociology of Terrorism. Annual Review of Sociology 2004:271-286.

(45) Federal Bureau of investigation. Domestic Terrorism, Tips Lead to Sting, Prison For Plotter, FBI Archives. 2018.

(46) Terry RA. Operation Rescue. Whitaker House Springdale, PA; 1988.

(47) Simi P, Smith L, Reeser AM. From Punk Kids to Public Enemy Number One. Deviant Behav 2008;29(8):753-774.

(48) Russell T. Republic of New Africa. Encyclopedia of African-American Culture and History. Encyclopedia.Com. 2005.

(49) Southern Poverty Law Center. Sovereign Citizens Movement. 2012.

(50) Weir JP. Sovereign Citizens: A Reasoned Response to the Madness. Lewis & Clark L Rev 2015;19(3):829.

(51) Gunter B, Nelson L. Alaska Militia Leader's Revolution Falls Flat. 2011.

(52) Lambert L. Symbionese Liberation Army: American Militant Group. 2017.

(53) Smith BL. Terrorism in America: Pipe Bombs and Pipe Dreams. SUNY Press; 1994.

(54) Hoffman B. Terrorism in the United States and the Potential Threat to Nuclear Facilities. Rand Santa Monica, CA; 1986.

(55) Lambert L. Weather Underground: American Militant Group. 2017.

(56) Potok M. the Year in Hate and Extremism. 2017.

(57) Horsley RA. the Sicarii: Ancient Jewish" Terrorists". the Journal of Religion 1979;59(4):435-458.

(58) Burke J. Al Qaeda. Foreign Policy 2004:18-26.

(59) Baker P, Cooper H, Mazzetti M. Bin Laden Is Dead, Obama Says. The New York Times 2011;1(5):2011.

(60) Stathis GM. ISIS, Syria, and Iraq: The Beginning of a Fourth Gulf War? Critical Issues in Justice and Politics 2015:1.

(61) Kenber B. Nidal Hasan Sentenced to Death for Fort Hood Shooting Rampage. Washington Post. 2013.

(62) Berrebi C. Evidence About the Link Between Education, Poverty and Terrorism Among Palestinians. Peace Economics, Peace Science and Public Policy 2007;13(1).

(63) Krueger AB, Malečková J. Education, Poverty and Terrorism: Is there A Causal Connection? The Journal of Economic Perspectives 2003;17(4):119-144.

(64) Richardson C. Relative Deprivation theory in Terrorism: A Study of Higher Education and Unemployment as Predictors of Terrorism. Politics Department, New York University 2011.

(65) Russell CA, Miller BH. Profile of A Terrorist. Studies in Conflict & Terrorism 1977;1(1):17-34.

(66) Sageman M. Understanding Terror Networks. University of Pennsylvania Press; 2004.

(67) Bureau of Labor Statistics. Labor Force Statistics from the Current Population Survey. 2018.

(68) Hassan N. An Arsenal of Believers: Talking To the "Human Bombs". the New Yorker 2001; 19:12/9/2018.

(69) Krueger AB, Laitin DD. Kto Kogo? A Cross-Country Study of the Origins and Targets of Terrorism. Terrorism, Economic

Development, and Political Openness 2008:148-173.

(70) De Mesquita EB. The Quality of Terror. Am J Polit Sci 2005;49(3):515-530.

(71) Burgoon B. On Welfare and Terror: Social Welfare Policies and Politicaleconomic Roots of Terrorism. Journal of Conflict Resolution 2006;50(2):176.

(72) Kis-Katos K, Liebert H, Schulze GG. On the Origin of Domestic and international Terrorism. European Journal of Political Economy 2011;27: S17-S36.

(73) États-Unis. Président (2001-20 (1) Federal Bureau of investigation. Terrorism 2002-2005. 2016.(71) Burgoon B. On Welfare and Terror: Social Welfare Policies and Politicaleconomic Roots of Terrorism. Journal of Conflict Resolution 2006;50(2):176.

(72) Kis-Katos K, Liebert H, Schulze GG. On the Origin of Domestic and international Terrorism. European Journal of Political Economy 2011;27: S17-S36.

(73) États-Unis. Président (2001-2009: Bush), Bush GW. Public Papers of the Presidents of the United States, George W. Bush. Office of the Federal Register, National Archives and Records Administration; 2003.

(74) Han C, Janmaat JG, Hoskins B, Green A. Perceptions of inequalities: Implications for Social Cohesion. London: Centre For Learning and Life Chances in Knowledge Economies and Societies 2012.

(75) Blumer H. Social Problems as Collective Behavior. Soc Probl 1971;18(3):298-306.

(76) Chen D. Economic Distress and Religious intensity: Evidence from Islamic Resurgence During the indonesian Financial

Crisis. Am Econ Rev 2003.

(77) Li Q, Schaub D. Economic Globalization and Transnational Terrorism A Pooled Time-Series Analysis. J Conflict Resolut 2004;48(2):230-258.

(78) Gurr TR. Why Men Rebel. 40th Anniversary Edition Ed. New York: Taylor & Francis; 2010.

(79) Abadie A. Poverty, Political Freedom, and the Roots of Terrorism. National Bureau of Economic Research 2004.

(80) Ranstorp M. Terrorism in the Name of Religion. J int Aff 1996:41-62.

(81) Southern Poverty Law Center. Antigovernment Movement. 2017.

(82) Beirich H, Buchanan S. 2017: The Year in Hate and Extremism. 2018

(83) Horn SF. Invisible Empire: the Story of the Ku Klux Klan, 1866-1871. Patterson Smith Publishing Corporation; 1969.

(84) Southern Poverty Law Center. Hate Map. 2016.

(85) Feder J. Racial Profiling: Legal and Constitutional Issues. 2012.

(86) Thomas III GC. Terrorism, Race and A New Approach to Consent Searches. Miss.LJ 2003;73:525.

(87) Gonzalez-Perez M. Women and Terrorism: Female Activity in Domestic and international Terror Groups. Routledge; 2008.

(88) Ferguson N, Binks E. Understanding Radicalization and Engagement in Terrorism Through Religious Conversion Motifs. Journal of Strategic Security 2015 Spring;8(1):16-26.

(89) Piazza JA. Rooted in Poverty? Terrorism, Poor Economic Development, and Social Cleavages 1. Terrorism and Political Violence 2006;18(1):159-177.

(90) Azam J, Thelen V. the Roles of Foreign Aid and Education in the War On Terror. Public Choice 2008;135(3-4):375-397.

(91) Almond K. Somalis Finding their Place in Minnesota. 2017.

(92) Nacos BL. The Portrayal of Female Terrorists in the Media: Similar Framing Patterns in the News Coverage of Women in Politics and in Terrorism. Studies in Conflict & Terrorism 2005;28(5):435-451.

(93) Dobson C, Payne R. the Carlos Complex: A Study in Terror. Putnam New York; 1977.

(94) Galvin DM. The Female Terrorist: A Socio-Psychological Perspective. Behav Sci Law 1983;1(2):19-32.

(95) Sjoberg L, Gentry CE. Women, Gender, and Terrorism. University of Georgia Press; 2011.

(96) Reif LL. Women in Latin American Guerrilla Movements: A Comparative Perspective. Comparative Politics 1986;18(2):147-169.

(97) Georges-Abeyie DE. Women as Terrorists. Perspectives on Terrorism. Wilmington, Delaware: Scholarly Resources 1983.

(98) Margolis DR. Women's Movements Around the World: Cross-Cultural Comparisons. Gender Soc 1993;7(3):379-399.

(99) Griset PL, Mahan S. Terrorism in Perspective. Sage Publications London; 2003.

(100) Kampwirth K. Women and Guerrilla Movements: Nicara-

gua, El Salvador, Chiapas, Cuba. Penn State Press; 2002.

(101) Yesevi CG. Female Terrorism. European Scientific Journal 2014;10(14):579.

(102) Dentice DE. Pseudo-Religion, White Spaces, and the Knights Party: A Case Study. Geographies of Religions and Belief Systems 2014;4(1):1-24.

(103) Rogers J, Litt J. Normalizing Racism: A Case Study of Motherhood in White Supremacy. Home-Grown Hate: Gender and Organized Racism, Edited By A. Ferber. Routledge: London 2004:97-112.

(104) Ferber AL. Home-Grown Hate: Gender and Organized Racism. Psychology Press; 2004.

(105) Wright L. One Drop of Blood. The New Yorker 1994; 25:46-55.

(106) Shakur A. Assata: An Autobiography. Zed Books; 1987.

(107) Powers T. Diana: The Making of a Terrorist. Houghton Mifflin; 1971.

(108) IBID

(109) Egan T. Is Abortion Violence A Plot? Conspiracy Is Not Confirmed. (Cover Story). New York Times 1995 06/18;144(50096):1.

(110) Robbins J. Report: Released Abortion-Clinic Terrorist to Take Up Residence in Douglas County. 2018.

(111) Stern S, Browder L. With the Weathermen: The Personal Journal of A Revolutionary Woman. Rutgers University Press; 2007.

(112) Blomberg SB, Hess GD, Weerapana A. Economic Condi-

tions and Terrorism. European Journal of Political Economy 2004;20(2):463-478.

(113) Bush GW. The National Security Strategy of the United States of America 2002.

(114) Rae J. Will It Ever Be Possible to Profile the Terrorist? Journal of Terrorism Research 2012;3(2).

(115) Jenkins BM. The Terrorist Mindset and Terrorist Decision-making: Two Areas of Ignorance. Terrorism 1980;3(3-4):245-250.

(116) Dingley J. the Terrorist-Developing A Profile. International Journal of Risk Security and Crime Prevention, 1997;2:25-37.

(117) Holman MR, Merolla JL, Zechmeister EJ. Sex, Stereotypes, and Security: A Study of the Effects of Terrorist Threat on Assessments of Female Leadership. Journal of Women, Politics & Policy 2011;32(3):173-192.

(118) Jacques K, Taylor PJ. Male and Female Suicide Bombers: Different Sexes, Different Reasons? Studies in Conflict & Terrorism 2008;31(4):304-326.

(119) Gardner E. Is there Method to the Madness? Worldwide Press Coverage of Female Terrorists and Journalistic Attempts to Rationalize their involvement. Journalism Studies 2007;8(6):909-929.

(120) Gambetta D, Hertog S. Engineers of Jihad. 2007.

(121) Lykken DT. The Causes and Costs of Crime and A Controversial Cure. J Pers 2000;68(3):559-605.

(122) Osipov V, Ivakin Y. Terrorists: Statistical Profile. Information Fusion and Geographic information Systems: Springer;

2009. P. 241-250.

(123) Pape RA. The Strategic Logic of Suicide Terrorism. American Political Science Review 2003;97(03):343-361.

(124) Winkates J. Suicide Terrorism: Martyrdom for Organizational Objectives. Journal of Third World Studies 2006;23(1):87.

(125) Lombardi M, Ragab E, Chin V. Countering Radicalization and Violent Extremism Among Youth To Prevent Terrorism. IOS Press; 2014.

(126) Gerstenfeld PB, Grant DR. Crimes of Hate: Selected Readings. Sage; 2004.

(127) Bjørgo T. Processes of Disengagement from Violent Groups of the Extreme Right. Leaving Terrorism Behind: Routledge; 2008. P. 48-66.

(128) Blazak R. White Boys to Terrorist Men: Target Recruitment of Nazi Skinheads. Am Behav Sci 2001;44(6):982-1000.

(129) Harper FE. To Kill the Messenger: The Deflection of Responsibility Through Scapegoating (A Socio-Legal Analysis of Parental Responsibility Laws and the Urban Gang Family). Harv. Blackletter J. 1991; 8:41.

(130) Volkan V. Blind Trust: Large Groups and their Leaders in Times of Crisis and Terror. Pitchstone Publishing (US&CA); 2014.

(131) Zawodny JK. Infrastructures of Terrorist Organizations. Journal of Conflict Studies 1981;1(4).

(132) Gerstenfeld PB, Grant DR. Crimes of Hate: Selected Readings Sage; 2004.

(133) Kao E. The Crisis of Fatherless Shooters. 2018.

(134) Kruglanski AW, Chen X, Golec A. Individual Motivations, the Group Process and Organizational Strategies in Suicide Terrorism. Journal of Policing, intelligence and Counter Terrorism 2008;3(1):70-84.

(135) Ginges J. Deterring the Terrorist: A Psychological Evaluation of Different Strategies for Deterring Terrorism. Terrorism and Political Violence 1997;9(1):170-185.

(136) Post JM. Notes on A Psychodynamic theory of Terrorist Behavior. 1984.

(137) Kellner D. Guys and Guns Amok: Domestic Terrorism and School Shootings from the Oklahoma City Bombing to the Virginia Tech Massacre. Routledge; 2015.

(138) Ozeren S, Gunes ID, Al-Badayneh DM. Understanding Terrorism: Analysis of Sociological and Psychological Aspects. IOS Press; 2007.

(139) Staub E. Preventing Violence and Terrorism and Promoting Positive Relations Between Dutch and Muslim Communities in Amsterdam. Peace and Conflict: Journal of Peace Psychology 2007;13(3):333-360.

(140) Richards J. Terrorism in Europe: The Local Aspects of a Global Threat. Jihadmonitor. Org; 2007.

(141) Mills G, Herbst J. Africa, Terrorism and AFRICOM. The RUSI Journal 2007;152(2):40-45.

(142) Schwartz SJ. A New Identity for Identity Research: Recommendations for Expanding and. J Adolesc Res 2005;20(3):293-308.

(143) Hamm MS. Prisoner Radicalization: Assessing the Threat in US Correctional institutions. NIJ Journal 2008; 261:14-19.

(144) Corner E, Gill P. A False Dichotomy? Mental Illness and Lone-Actor Terrorism. Law Hum Behav 2015;39(1):23.

(145) Hoffman B. "Holy Terror": The Implications of Terrorism Motivated by A Religious Imperative. Studies in Conflict & Terrorism 1995;18(4):271-284.

(146) Juergensmeyer M. Terror in the Mind of God: The Global Rise of Religious Violence.: Taylor & Francis; 2005.

(147) Pratt D. Religion and Terrorism: Christian Fundamentalism and Extremism. Terrorism and Political Violence 2010;22(3):438-456.

(148) Terrorism and Terroristic Threats - Findlaw. (149) Hong N. Are Terrorists Ready for Life After Prison? Wall Street Journal (Online) 2018.

(150) See S. Returning Foreign Terrorist Fighters: A Catalyst for Recidivism Among Disengaged Terrorists. Counter Terrorist Trends and Analyses 2018;10(6):7-15.

(151) Prunty L. the Terrorist Expatriation Act: Unconstitutional and Unnecessary-How the Proposed Legislation Is Unconstitutional and Redundant. JCR & Econ.Dev. 2011;26:1009.

(152) Speckhard A. Prison and Community-Based Disengagement and De-Radicalization Programs for Extremist involved in Militant Jihadi Terrorism Ideologies and Activities. Psychosocial, Organizational and Cultural Aspects of Terrorism 2011:1-14.

(153) Horgan J, Altier MB. The Future of Terrorist De-Radicalization Programs. Georgetown Journal of international Affairs 2012:83-90.

(154) Kearney S. Anger Management to Avert Would-Be Terrorists. Australian, the 2005.

(155) Horgan J, Braddock K. Rehabilitating the Terrorists? Challenges in Assessing the Effectiveness of De-Radicalization Programs. Terrorism and Political Violence 2010;22(2):267-291.

(156) Holtmann P. Countering Al-Qaeda's Single Narrative. Perspectives on Terrorism 2013;7(2).

(157) Mealer MJ. internet Radicalization: Actual Threat or Phantom Menace? 2012.

(158) Ferguson JR. Biological Weapons and US Law. JAMA 1997;278(5):357-360.

(159) Clinton WJ. Executive Order 12947: Prohibiting Transactions with Terrorists Who Threaten to Disrupt the Middle East Peace Process. The Federal Register 1995.

(160) Dlin E. Antiterrorism and Effective Death Penalty Act of 1996: An Attempt to Quench Anti-Immigration Sentiments, the. Cath.Law. 1998; 38:49.

(161) Bush GW. Executive Order 13224—Blocking Property and Prohibiting Transactions with Persons Who Commit, Threaten to Commit, Or Support Terrorism. Fed Regist 2001; 66:186.

(162) the USA Patriot Act: A Sketch. DTIC Document; 2002.

(163) Congress U. Homeland Security Act of 2002. Public Law 2002;107.

(164) Bland SS. Section by Section Summary of Sensenbrenner Bill. VISALAW.COM: The Immigration Law Portal 2005.

(165) Suleman AM. Military Commissions Act of 2006. Harvard

Human Rights Journal 2007;20.

(166) Beard JM. The Geneva Boomerang: The Military Commissions Act of 2006 and US Counterterror Operations. Am J int Law 2007:56-73.

Index

Abdifatah Aden................................61, 66, 167
Abdirahman Sheik Mohamud....................66, 167
Abdulhakim Mujahid Muhammad 61, 165
Abdulrahman Farhane 51
Abu Dawuud 153
Adham Amin Hassoun 48
ADHD 134
AEDPA 198
Afghanistan...........48-49, 57, 67-68, 108, 152, 158, 160, 165-166
Ahmad Abousamra 49
Ahmed Bilal 52
Ahmed Ibrahim Bilal. 52
Air Force 151, 163
Alabama Free Militia 26
Alaska SC Cell 47
al-Awlaki.............60-61, 66, 97-98, 148, 155, 162
Albania 111-112
ALF...28, 32
Alfred P. Murrah Federal Building 22, 42
Al Fuqra 56-58, 105, 120, 133, 136
Al Haramain Islamic Foundation 56-58, 133, 136
Allen Walter Lyon................................156
al-Nusra 21, 56-57, 66, 120, 133, 136, 155
Alpha 66 and Omega 26
al-Qaeda..18,21,33,49-50,52,54,56-61,66,68,70,72,97,103,105-106,119-120,130,132-133,136,152,158,162,166,186,195-196,219
Al-Qaida in the Arabian Peninsula 56, 60, 97
al-Shabaab ..21, 56-57, 61-62, 70, 105, 119-121, 133, 136, 162, 188
Alt-right 26, 89, 132
Aman Hassan Yemer 48, 135
Anes Subasic 51

Animal Liberation Front 28
Ansar al-Islam 56-57, 62, 133, 136
Anthony Hayne...41, 184
Anti-government 24, 40, 88
Antonio Martinez...167
Antonio Veciana Blanch 27
Anwar al-Awlaki 60-61, 66, 97, 148, 155, 162
Arkansas 61, 165, 190
Army 29-31, 35, 42,
60, 64, 67, 114-115, 117, 124-126, 147-149, 151-158, 168, 206-209
Army National Guard 148, 152, 155-157
Army of God.....................................29-30, 125-126, 206-207
Army of the Righteous.. 67
Assault 52, 155, 161, 164, 166, 176
Barack Obama 32, 88-90, 130, 195, 199
Bilal Abood 151
Bill Ayres...43, 124
Bill (William) Clinton 32, 43, 88, 197
Biological Weapons 172, 196-197, 219
Bipolar disorder..134
Black Liberation Army 30-31, 35, 124, 207-208
Bobby Seale..30
Bomb... 31, 33-
34, 41-42, 49, 69, 123-124, 132, 151, 154, 160, 167, 172, 184-185
Bombs 22, 89, 121, 154, 172, 187, 190, 205, 209-210
Border Protection, Anti-terrorism, and Illegal Immigration Control
Act of 2005.. 201
Born Again 94, 100
Brandon Baxter...183
Brian Neal Vinas...158
Bronx...50, 63
Brooklyn...48, 103, 126, 183
Brooklyn Bridge.. 48, 183

Buffalo Six...49, 68, 103
Burson Augustin...50
California.....................28-30, 33, 42-43, 97, 103, 148, 154, 160
Calvin Jones...34
Canada.....................................27-28, 58, 157
Caribbean.......................................58, 111-112
Carlos Leon Bledsoe.......................................61, 165
Cesar Sayoc...89
CFR...18, 188
Charles Bishop...186
Chemical weapons.................................17, 172, 199
China...40, 109, 112
Christian Identity.................................30-31, 36, 207
Christopher Paul...47
CIA...27
Cincinnati...164
Clark Calloway...159
Cleveland.....................................41, 101, 132, 164, 183
Clifford L. Cousins...135
Coleman Barney...47
Columbus.................................47, 60, 66, 101, 105
Columbus Terror Cell.......................................47, 105
Connor Stevens...184
Conspiracy to commit murder.............................51, 156
Craig Benedict Baxam.......................................152
Crimes Involving Violence.................................185
Cryptology...152
Cuba.................................27, 40, 124, 206, 214
Cuban Nationalist Movement...............................27
Cuban National Liberation Front.............................27
Curtis Culwell Center...51
Daniel Aljughaifi...49
Daniel Boyd...51, 165

Daniel Joseph Maldonado 49
Daniel Koehler 194
Daniel Seth Franey 153
David Headley 68, 135
David Wright 41, 47
D.C. Five 48, 103
Decarus Lowell Thomas 51
Democrats 151
Denver 153-154
Department of Homeland Security 111, 195, 201
Depression 134
De-Radicalization 194, 218-219
Detainee Treatment Act of 2005 201
Disengagement 189, 191, 194, 216, 218
DOD 17, 19
Donald DeFreeze 42-43
Donald T. Surratt 160
Douglas Wright 183
Dylan Boyd 51, 165
Earth Liberation Front 28, 31-32, 206, 208
Eduardo Arocena 27
Egypt 65, 108, 155, 163
Elton Simpson 51
Emerson Begolly 135
Eric Harroun 155
Esteban Santiago 157
Everett Aaron Jameson 159
Executive Order 12947 .... 197, 219
Executive Order 13224 .... 199, 219
Fake news 15
FALN 32
Farah Mohamed Beledi 62
Faysal Galab 49

FBI 17-18, 20-21, 31, 37-38, 40, 43, 47-50, 52-53, 59, 62, 89, 120, 123-124, 151, 153-156, 158-162, 165, 167-168, 179-180, 183-185, 188, 197, 209

Federal Bureau of Investigation17-18, 179, 197, 205-206, 209, 211

Federal Policies.. 192, 195

Filiberto Ojeda Rios... 32

Financing of Terrorism... 171

Florida............................. 27, 34, 48, 60, 64, 105, 186

Florida Cell 48

Fort Dix...48-49, 125, 167

Fort Hood 60, 98, 155, 210

Fort Lewis 154

France 109, 111

Frank O. McCord..34

Frederick Domingue Jr. 166

Ft. Hood 151

Fuerzas Armadas de Liberacion Nacional Puertorriquena 32

Gaza 63, 109, 112

Ghana.. 109, 112

George W. Bush 82, 88, 157, 195, 199, 201

Gregory Hubbard...159

Gregory Vernon Patterson................................33, 167

Guantanamo 183, 187, 194, 201

Hallucinations 134, 161

Hamas....................56-57, 62-63, 81, 133, 136, 158

Hammad Abdur-Raheem 53, 156

Hammad Riaz Samana 33

Harlem Suarez 134

Hasan Akbar 135, 152

Hasan Edmonds 153

Hassan Abu-Jihaad 161

Hate crime 20, 205

Hezbollah................... 56-57, 63-64, 120, 133, 136

Hillary Clinton 90
Hizballah..63
Holocaust...163
Homeland Security Act of 2002 ....196, 201, 219
hostage taking...163
Huey Newton 30, 207
Hysen Sherifi 51
Ikaika Erik Kang..156
Iran.. 57-58, 64, 111
Iraq..
54, 56-57, 60-62, 64, 65, 70, 111, 120, 133, 136, 157, 160, 166, 210
ISIS 21, 47,
49, 52, 54, 56-57, 59, 64, 65, 70, 72, 74, 103-106, 119-120, 122,
130, 132-133, 136, 153, 156-157, 159, 162-164, 185, 194, 196, 210
Islamic State of Iraq 54, 56, 61, 64, 65, 70, 120, 133, 136
Islamic State of Iraq and the Levant 64, 65, 70
Israel 63, 65, 109, 111
Israeli 33, 63
Iyman Faris.. 47, 135, 183
Izz al-Din al-Qassam Brigade.. 63
Jaber Elbaneh..49
Jaish-e-Mohammed 56-57, 67, 133, 136
James Cromitie...50, 165
James Ellison...31
James Elshafay 135
James R. Crowe 34
James W. Von Brunn..163
Jam'iyyat Ul-Islam Is-Saheeh 33, 132
Jason Michael Ludke...134
JDL.. 34, 120
Jeffrey Leon Battle...52, 152
Jesse Morton 195
Jewish Defense League..................... 34, 45, 105, 119-120, 132

Jibreel 159
Jihadist Cell 49
Jim David Adkisson...151
JIS 33
John Allen Muhammad..156
John B. Kennedy..34
John C. Lester 34
Joseph Anthony Davis 161, 166
Joshua Cummings 153
Joshua Stafford..184
Karen Vernon... 47
Kassem Daher 48
Kenya 109, 111, 153
Keto..94
Kevin James...33, 167
Kevin William Harpham 154
Khalid Sheikh Mohammed...183
Kifah Jayyousi 48, 162
KKK.. 34-35, 90, 122-123, 208
Ku Klux Klan.................... 34, 90, 114, 121-123, 208, 212
Kuwait...111, 163-164
Kyrgyzstan 109, 112
Lackawanna Six 49, 68, 103
Laguerre Payen.. 50, 166
Lashkar-e-Taiba..158
Lashkar-e-Tayyiba.............................. 56-57, 67, 133, 136
Laundering of monetary instruments 174
Lebanon 52, 57, 63, 65, 108, 110
Levar Haley Washington 167
Liberty Seven 105
Libya 109, 111-112
Little Rock.. 61, 165
Los Angeles 33, 154, 157, 167

Lyglenson Lemorin...50
M19CO 35-36
Maher Hawash..52
Mahin Khan 134
Mahud Faruq Brent..51
Making false statements... 53, 162, 172
Marine... 51, 159-160, 165
Marines 151, 154, 158-160, 164
Martin Luther King Jr 154
Marwan Othman El-Hindi 52, 166
Maryland..153
Material support.. 23,
49, 64, 67, 69, 105, 120, 155-159, 163, 166, 170-171, 188, 190-191
Matthew Aaron Llaneza 160
May 19th Communist Organization 35-36
Mexico..97, 105, 109, 112, 148
Miami.. 50, 60, 105
Miami Seven 50
Micah Johnson 20
Michael Anderson... 47
Michael Bray 29
Military 33, 49, 53, 61, 63, 66-69, 75, 89, 125, 132, 147-156, 158-
159, 161, 164-168, 183-185, 191, 195, 198, 201, 205, 207, 219-220
Mohamed Amiin Ali Roble...134
Mohamed Bailor Jalloh 61, 155
Mohammad Omar Aly Hassan...51
Mohammad Youssuf Abdulazeez 134
Mohammad Zaki Amawi 52, 166
Money laundering... 158, 174
Muhammad Ibrahim Bilal.. 52
Muhammed Taheri-Azar 135
Muktar Al-Bakri..49
Murder 20, 29-30, 35,

43, 45, 51, 79, 89, 124-126, 152, 156, 158, 162, 164-165, 171, 190

Muslim ....

48, 51, 58-59, 63, 67, 94, 132, 148, 158, 161, 165, 195, 205, 217

Nadir Hamid Soofi 51

Narseal Batiste 50

Naser Jason Abdo 151

Nasser al-Awlaki 97

National Alliance 36, 42

National Guard 50, 64, 148, 152, 155-157, 165

National Youth Alliance 36

Naudimar Herrera 50

Naveed Afzal Haq 135

Navy 151, 161-164

Newburgh Four... 50, 103, 165

New Jersey...27, 49, 106, 124, 168, 185, 190

New Mexico 97, 148

New York 27, 34, 49, 51, 60, 68-69, 74, 101-103,

113, 121, 123-124, 163, 180, 183, 185, 190, 199, 205, 210, 212-214

New York City..............................51, 60, 69, 101, 163, 199, 205

Nicaragua...109, 112, 115, 213

Nicholas Michael Teausant 157

Nicholas Rovinski... 47

Nidal Hasan 60-61, 98, 151, 155, 164, 210

Nuclear terrorism 172

Nuradin Abdi 47

Nusra Front 56-57, 66-67, 120, 133, 136

NY Terror Cell...51

Obama.. 32, 88-90, 130, 195, 199, 210

Obstruction of justice 174

Occupy Wall Street 41, 132, 154

October Martinique 52, 79, 118

Official Charges...170

Ohio.................... 37, 43, 60, 64, 66, 101, 105, 132, 164, 167, 183

Omega 7 26-27
Onta Williams 50, 165
Operation Save America 37
Oregon 28, 60
Osama bin Laden 48-49, 58-59, 148, 161
Paddock 16
Pakistan ... 51, 56-59, 67-69, 81, 107-108, 110, 133, 136, 158, 165
Pakistani Five 48, 103
Palestine.. 63, 65, 108
Palestinian 57, 62-63
Pamela Geller... 47
Panama 109, 112
Parade 154
Patrice Lumumba Ford 52
Patrick Abraham..50
Patty Hearst..43
Paul Hall 161, 164
PEN1 39
Perry nuclear power plant 164
Phineas Priesthood.. 38
Plastic Explosives 172, 198
Portland 52, 60, 79, 150, 152
Portland Seven.......................... 52, 79, 150, 152
Post-traumatic stress disorder 134, 157, 160
Prevention Strategies 192
Prison Location...180
Profiling 90-91, 138-139, 202, 212
Prophet Muhammad 52
PTSD 150
Public Enemy Number 1..................................139
Puerto Rican 45
Quantico..51, 165
Rabbi Meir Kahane..34

Rafiq Abdus Sabiur..51
Ramy Zamzam..48
Randall Blue Chapman...158
Randell Terry...37
Rasel Raihan...134
Raymond Luc Levasseur. 43
Rene Wright..51
Republic of New Africa..35, 40, 209
Revolutionary People's Group.............40-41, 53, 105, 132, 183
Rezwan Ferdaus...89, 135
Richard Girnt Butler..30
Richard Henry..40
Richard R. Reed...34
Right Wing...24
RNA..35, 40
Robert Goldstein..34
Roe vs. Wade..29
Roger Stockham 135, 157
Rothschild Augustine 50
Sahim Alwan..49
Santos Colon Jr..135
Saudi Arabia 57-58, 65, 194
Schaeffer Cox 42, 47
Seattle 126, 161, 166
Second World War...54
Seifullah..53, 158
Sensenbrenner Bill 201, 219
Sentencing 126, 135, 154, 159, 170, 180-182
Shafal Mosed 49
Shariah..62, 67-68
Sharia law 20, 66, 155
Sicarii 54, 209
Sierra Leone..109, 111

Silvia Baraldini 35
SLA..42-43
Somalia 57, 62, 105, 107-108, 110-112, 160, 188
Sovereign Citizens 41-42,47, 209
Spokane 154
Sri Lanka.. 69, 109, 112, 114
Stanley Grant Phanor 50
Stephen Paddock 16
Sudan 111
Syed Hashmi..166
Symbionese Liberation Army..42, 209
Syria 49, 54, 56-58,
64, 65-67, 93, 110-111, 120, 133, 136, 151, 155, 159, 163, 167, 210
Tahmeed Ahmad, ...135
Tairod Nathan Webster Pugh..163
Taliban 52, 56-57, 68-69, 120, 133, 136, 152, 155, 160-161
Tamil Tigers.............................. 56-57, 69, 114, 133, 136
Tarek Mehanna...49
Tarik Shah...51
Tehrik-e-Taliban..69
Texas 20, 38, 49, 51-52, 60, 64, 105, 151, 155, 186
Texas Cartoon Terrorists.. 51
The Biological Weapons Anti-Terrorism Act of 1989.............196
The Black Panther Party....................................... 30, 124, 207
The Covenant, the Sword, and the Arm of the Lord 31, 208
The DC Sniper...156
The Jewish Defense League 34, 45, 105
The National Socialist Movement 36
Theophilus Burroughs..63, 158
Timeline..121
Toledo 37, 52, 60, 105, 121, 166
Toledo Terror Cell..52, 105, 166
Torrance Four 33, 167

Torture 201
Trump 88-90, 110, 195
Twitter...123, 151
UFF 43
Umar Farooq 48
United Freedom Front... 43
United States 17-18,
20, 22, 28, 32, 39-40, 46, 48, 54, 58, 60, 63, 82, 90, 93, 117,
149-150, 163, 165, 168, 172-174, 197, 199, 205, 207, 209, 211, 215
Usaama Abdullah Rahim 47
USA PATRIOT Act.................... 171, 196, 199-200, 219
USA FreedomAct 199
Use of weapons of mass destruction 172
Uzbekistan 109, 112
Variola virus...172
VBIED 62
Vegan 94
Veteran.. 151, 157, 160
Vietnam.................................... 122, 124, 152, 157
Virginia ..V, 48, 53, 68, 97, 103, 150, 155-156, 158, 160, 207, 217
Walli Mujahidh 135, 166
Wall Street 41, 132, 154, 218
Waqar Hassan Khan..48
Washington...
33-34, 40, 60, 64, 112, 126, 154, 161, 163, 166-167, 185, 206, 210
Wassim I. Mazloum...166
Weapons 6-17, 42, 47, 63, 121, 152, 158, 160-161,
163, 166-167, 171-173, 186-187, 190-191, 196-197, 199-200, 219
Weather Underground Organization ... 35, 43, 122, 124, 126-127
West Bank.. 63
White Supremacist 38, 41, 89-90, 119, 123, 127, 163
White Supremacy 39, 214
William Pierce 36

WMD..172
World Trade Center...22, 93
WUO 43-44, 125, 127
Yahya Goba 49
Yasein Taher 49
Yemen 50, 60, 68, 97, 108, 111, 148
Yonathan Melaku...................................89, 135, 160
Younus Abdullah Muhammad 195
Zakariya Boyd..165
Zale H. Thompson 162
Ziyad Yaghi 51